Creating the Engine for
Transformational Sales Results

ERIK THERWANGER

DYNAMIC SALES COMBUSTION

Creating the Engine for Transformational Sales Results

The
ThinkGREAT®
COLLECTION

BALBOA.
PRESS
A DIVISION OF HAY HOUSE

Balboa Press books may be ordered through booksellers or by contacting:

Balboa Press
A Division of Hay House
1663 Liberty Drive
Bloomington, IN 47403
www.balboapress.com
1 (877) 407-4847

Because of the dynamic nature of the Internet, any web addresses or links contained in this book may have changed since publication and may no longer be valid. The views expressed in this work are solely those of the author and do not necessarily reflect the views of the publisher, and the publisher hereby disclaims any responsibility for them.

The author of this book does not dispense medical advice or prescribe the use of any technique as a form of treatment for physical, emotional, or medical problems without the advice of a physician, either directly or indirectly. The intent of the author is only to offer information of a general nature to help you in your quest for emotional and spiritual well-being. In the event you use any of the information in this book for yourself, which is your constitutional right, the author and the publisher assume no responsibility for your actions.

This book is a work of non-fiction. Unless otherwise noted, the author and the publisher make no explicit guarantees as to the accuracy of the information contained in this book and in some cases, names of people and places have been altered to protect their privacy.

Any people depicted in stock imagery provided by Getty Images are models, and such images are being used for illustrative purposes only. Certain stock imagery © Getty Images.

Scripture taken from the King James Version of the Bible.

Print information available on the last page.

ISBN: 978-1-9822-1295-7 (sc)
ISBN: 978-1-9822-1297-1 (hc)
ISBN: 978-1-9822-1296-4 (e)

Library of Congress Control Number: 2018912292

Balboa Press rev. date: 11/21/2018

Dedicated to:

Everyone who told me "no" throughout my sales journey. My desire to earn your "yes" has helped me to become a Transformational Sales Leader.

Everyone who has "found" themselves in sales and is looking to "find" themselves in sales! Your desire to enhance your perception about selling, transform your sales results, and improve your life in the process, has made this book a reality.

The amazing sales professionals whom I have had the honor of working with; your unselfish ability to teach me the ropes, about sales and myself, has forever enhanced my life.

CONTENTS

THE 3 PILLARS

SUPPORTING YOUR GROWTH

Build - Strengthen - Expand

No matter what industry you are in, your organization is supported by three distinct disciplines - leadership, strategic planning, and sales performance. A structural break, in any single pillar, can significantly impact your ability to fulfill your mission and achieve your vision.

The 3 Pillars of Business Greatness provide you with the resources to unify all three, increasing their strength and providing the support and structure necessary to exceed your goals. Unique to the business world, these three essential programs will unify your people, with a shared dialogue, and create the greatest levels of structure, synergy, and success.

Developing your leaders, creating your strategic plan, and enhancing your sales system should not be taken lightly. Each book, *The LEADERSHIP Connection*, *ELEVATE*, and *Dynamic Sales COMBUSTION* forms a collective cohesion of strategies and techniques for greater results.

Welcome to Pillar 3... Selling!

Dynamic Sales Combustion will introduce you and your team to a new way of selling; one that unleashes their true potential. By looking at sales as the engine of your business, you will begin creating high-performance sales combustion and achieve transformational sales results.

It's time to remove the roadblocks from your path and accelerate your entire sales team. You will enhance your sales vehicle and drive your sales efforts in the direction you have always dreamed of, and perhaps a bit further!

INTRODUCTION

LEADERS, START YOUR SALES ENGINES!

Transforming Your Results.

There is no denying that *sales* is not the dream career people typically strive for. But I'm sure you already knew that. According to the Bureau of Labor Statistics, however, there are more than 14 million sales-related jobs in the US and millions more that support sales efforts. It is undeniably the lifeblood of nearly every organization and yet most sales people never anticipated being in that role, let alone making a career in sales.

As children, we share dreams of becoming doctors, astronauts, actors, singers, or professional athletes. Not one of my childhood friends ever said, "When I grow up, I want to sell..." insurance, used cars, cell phones, or anything else for that matter. I know that it never entered my mind.

In most high school yearbooks, you will find the "Most Likely To..." categories: Most likely to succeed, get married first, make a difference in the world, run off with the circus, or win the lottery. The list goes on and on and I have never seen, "Most Likely to Sell." I certainly would not have been in that category. If anything, I would have fallen into the "Least Likely to Sell" section.

As a child, I loved going to the movies with my father. I grew up on Indiana Jones, Star Wars, and all of the great '80s action films. It is no secret that I have always been a huge Arnold Schwarzenegger fan and I even ditched school to see him awarded his star on the Hollywood Walk of Fame. I had two dreams in high school and selling was not one of them. One was to become a filmmaker and the other was to serve our nation.

With six months remaining in high school, I enlisted in the United States Marine Corps and waited until graduation to ship out. I raised my right hand, took the oath, and began the Marine Corps on-boarding program - boot camp. After graduating as a Marine, I was trained as an air traffic controller and stationed at Marine Corps Air Station, Yuma, Arizona.

With one year left on my tour of duty, war had been declared and Operation Desert Storm was launched. We immediately began to train in the Yuma desert, going on forced marches that stretched for miles. It was August and the sun scorched us at nearly 120 degrees. As if that wasn't bad enough, our leaders prepared us for the chemical warfare tactics, promised by Saddam Hussein, and launched gas canisters to test our skills with our gas masks.

Just before deploying to the Middle East, I received a message from the Red Cross. My father was gravely ill and they recommended that I be sent home to be at his side. This was one of the hardest decisions of my life. I wanted to be with my father, but also wanted to be with my Marine brothers as we shipped out. Ultimately, the decision was made for me. My Gunnery Sergeant arranged for a transfer to Marine Corps Air Station, El Toro, California.

My father was still in a coma due to his diabetes. But miraculously he pulled through and I watched the war unfold from El Toro. It was reassuring to see my fellow troops return home, to a welcome far different than our service members received in our previous conflict - Vietnam. On Aug 23, 1991, I took my uniform off for the last time.

Honorably discharged from the Marines, it was time to return to my civilian life and move forward with becoming a filmmaker. I packed up my uniforms and prepared for my new journey. Using my G.I. Bill, I enrolled at Orange Coast College and began my studies. It was an incredible feeling to follow my passion and head in the direction of my dreams.

I embraced every aspect of my new path and completed my two-year degree in one year and eight months and did it with a 4.0

GPA. Not only had I become the Valedictorian, but I was asked to be the graduation speaker. I was also accepted to the University of Southern California to begin their Cinema/Television program. Everything seemed a bit surreal as I moved closer and closer to my goals.

During my studies at USC, I met the girl of my dreams, Gina. We began dating and soon after, I was offered the opportunity to begin working in the post-production side of the entertainment business. I accepted a position at Pacific Ocean Post, a state-of-the-art editorial and special effects company. I started in 1996 as a manager for their film and video vault as they worked on the digital effects shots for a "little" movie called Independence Day.

Flash forward two years to 1998 and Gina had accepted my marriage proposal. On Halloween, after dating for three years, we tied the knot. We had an amazing wedding, complete with a costume-party reception. Gina and I were excited to start our life together and one of the best parts was that I was not doing anything even remotely close to selling. At least not yet!

WHY SALES?

Why did you choose sales? I remember the exact moment I chose sales, or it chose me. It was more of a last resort than a career choice. I had absolutely loved my *non–sales* position in the entertainment industry, but that was short-lived. Like most newlyweds, Gina and I set exciting goals to buy a home, start a family, and travel the world. Have you ever set a goal, but life threw you a curve ball and made it tough to accomplish?

A curve ball was hurled at us just ten months after we were married. Gina visited her doctor and heard three words that changed our lives forever... "You have cancer." It was stage 3 Non-Hodgkin's Lymphoma and we were told that it was growing very aggressively. Her oncologist prepared to start chemotherapy immediately and our goals quickly began to fade as we focused only on Gina's situation.

The next few days seemed like a blur and she was scheduled for her first cycle of chemotherapy. As they prepared her for the treatment, her oncologist pulled me aside and encouraged me to, "Keep Gina positive; keep her spirits high," he said. Simple enough, right?

At first, it seemed easy to think about being Gina's source of positivity - her cheerleader to keep her in the right mindset. But it proved more difficult than I had anticipated as the realities of her diagnosis became evident. The chemotherapy alone caused her to become violently ill. She would undergo seven cycles of this treatment over the next twenty-one weeks, which ultimately had no effect on the cancer.

Immediately after her diagnosis, Gina went onto disability and we would soon feel the tightening financial stress. I also knew that I did not have the time to drive through Los Angeles each day, work a full-time job, commute home, and fulfill the role of a caregiver. So, I searched for alternate career options and discovered an opportunity that appeared to provide me with the ability to control my time and income. This was exactly what we needed.

The financial services industry required me to pass a few tests to become a licensed financial consultant. But there was a huge downside... it was all sales. Without a shred of sales training and with zero experience in the financial services arena, I had a life-changing decision to make. To make matters more difficult, I would not receive a salary, just commission.

What was I thinking? Being in sales was foreign to me and I had a lot at stake, including my orders to keep Gina positive. I was the worst possible candidate for this type of job and I knew it. But what if it worked? I sat on the edge of Gina's hospital bed and made the decision to become "Most Likely to Sell." I pushed aside my hang-ups about selling and made a commitment to Gina to make this 'sales thing' work.

SALES VEHICLE

My new career was off to a slow start. Income was not coming in as I had hoped. Although the dreams of being a successful sales agent were within reach, selling was far tougher than I had anticipated. My truck was repossessed, and our electricity was shut off. I was not achieving the results I had hoped for and I was not providing my wife with positive thoughts.

Instead of being a top producer, I found myself becoming an expert at preparing Top Ramen. Yes, it was only ten cents per bag. But often, that was all we could afford to eat. We kept positive attitudes, as much as we could. But if I was going to make my sales journey work, I needed an edge. So, I tried desperately to learn the secrets of successful sales people.

I talked with the top agents in our office, intently studied sales books, and listened to inspirational seminars. I discovered that everyone in sales faced challenges, but some succeeded despite their difficulties. How do they do it? Some studies show that 8% of sales people generate up to 80% of the sales. I needed to be part of the 8%.

Successful sales people are "going somewhere" and selling is a way of arriving at their destinations. But most fail to effectively operate their *sales vehicle*. Instead of cruising to their goals, they sputter and stall, rarely achieving the acceleration needed to succeed. Their challenges are often greater than their vehicle's capabilities and when the "Check Engine Light" comes on, they quickly experience high levels of frustration.

SALES ENGINE

I may have started my sales career during less-than-optimal circumstances, but I could not afford to stall. I needed an engine to provide unlimited power to my vehicle. What if I could create a sustainable sales engine and experience dynamic sales combustion? I did! And by doing so, I did much more than just power my sales vehicle, I discovered my true potential.

I became a top producer in my office, led a team of agents, and even started my own general agency. I then pursued my original goals, going back into the post-production business, where I became the vice president of a media company in Southern California. I designed a sales department, built a sales team, and developed a sales system that not only achieved dynamic sales combustion, but grew our annual sales by more than 300%.

I may have been the "Least Likely to Sell," but I now train sales professionals across the country on the ground–breaking techniques in this book. *Dynamic Sales COMBUSTION* is more than just theories, it is an instruction manual to creating your own high-performance sales engine and achieving the transformational sales results you need.

By reading *Dynamic Sales COMBUSTION* you will:

- Learn how to develop an *Unbreakable MINDSET*
- Understand the importance of *Unparalleled DATA*
- Discover how to create *Unstoppable GEARS*
- Realize the strength of having *Unmatched STRUCTURE*

Regardless of your circumstances, you can always fire up your sales engine to improve to your performance and results. I know this because tough times did not end with Gina's first battle with cancer. She would be diagnosed three more times and later suffer cardiac arrest in 2016. In addition to surviving her health battles, she now helps me to run our company, Think GREAT. Together, with our team, we experience transformational sales results and help others to do the same.

If you are ready for new levels of success, *Dynamic Sales COMBUSTION* will introduce you to a transformational new way of selling, for you and your team. It's time to get in your vehicle, buckle up, and start your sales engine.

Think GREAT,

Erik

Sales Diagnostic

The Sales Impact System (SIS)

I build engines and attach wheels to them.

~ Enzo Ferrari

Sales Diagnostic

The Sales Impact System (SIS)

Inspecting Your Sales Vehicle.

There are few things we like less than taking our vehicles to an auto shop for repairs. According to AutoMD.com, "Most consumers (83%) rank the experience of going to the repair shop/dealership to get their car repaired on par with going to the dentist, with women preferring the dentist."

According to a recent survey from AAA, American drivers don't trust auto mechanics, finding that 66% of drivers do not trust car repair shops. The survey added that "one-third of U.S. drivers (75 million motorists in total) have yet to find a trusted repair facility, leaving them feeling vulnerable when trouble strikes," said John Nielsen, AAA's Managing Director of automotive engineering and repair.

Why is there such a high level of distrust? According to AAA, below are some of the top reasons:

76% feel the shop recommends unnecessary services.

73% believe the shop overcharges.

53% have had a negative experience with a shop.

49% are concerned that the work will not be done correctly.

The diagnosis of the vehicle has nearly been removed by the recommendation to merely replacing a part, see if that works, and replace another part if that fails. In the mind of the consumer, there is no focus on taking a close, detailed look at their engine. The lack of a diagnosis leads to mistrust. I have found that most sales leaders tend to enjoy going to the dentist more than taking a closer look at the performance of their own sales engine.

Just like any vehicle, your sales vehicle has two distinct sections: the body and the engine. The body holds everything, from passengers and manuals, to drink holders and tools. It also contains the other important section: the engine, which provides the power to move forward. Unfortunately, most sales leaders pay greater attention to the body - the appearance of their vehicle - than to the engine. But true success is found under the hood.

Many try to gloss over the performance issues in sales, hoping a coat of paint will give the appearance that everything is working. But the engine tells a different story. While most sales teams may require some body work, it's the performance of the engine that allows the vehicle to get things moving.

When I meet with sales leaders and ask about their individual performance or the production of their teams, they typically share everything that is going well. 'Our calls are up,' they say, or 'We have new appointments.' Or they acknowledge that they are hitting some of their numbers. They describe what looks good, like the exterior paint job or shiny rims.

As we dive deeper, it soon becomes evident that the performance of the engine is rarely functioning at the peak of its potential. The 450-horsepower engine sometimes struggles to even gallop. Most sales leaders know when their engine is not running properly. They can feel it. But without a detailed diagnostic, they struggle to identify the true issues, making it impossible to resolve them.

Without a proper diagnostic, sales leaders can experience unnecessary frustration, stress, and delays. They tend to solve problems by just replacing the parts and hoping one of them will be the right fit. The exhausting exercise of replacing parts rarely results in a high-performance engine. The "Check Engine Light" requires a closer look inside.

Even if your sales efforts are not yielding the results you are striving for, it is highly unlikely that your sales vehicle is "Totaled." A proper inspection of the engine will position you to better understand the adjustments needed to achieve higher performance.

Let's take a look at what's under your hood.

THE SALES IMPACT SYSTEM - SIS

Your sales results are far too important to leave things to chance or to hope for the best. Just as a vehicle's engine creates motion through the four cycles of internal combustion, the *Sales Impact System* will enhance your sales engine to achieve transformational results through the four cycles of *Dynamic Sales Combustion*.

The Four Cycles of an Internal Combustion Engine:

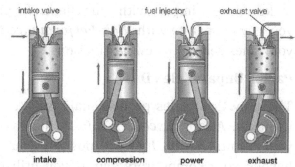

1. Intake

2. Compression

3. Power

4. Exhaust

The Four Cycles of *Dynamic Sales Combustion*:

1. Unbreakable MINDSET

2. Unparalleled DATA

3. Unstoppable GEARS

4. Unmatched STRUCTURE

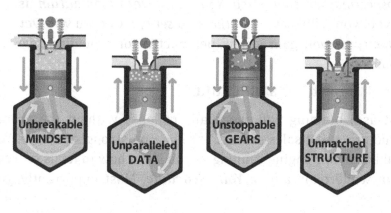

YOUR MANUAL FOR TRANSFORMATIONAL SALES RESULTS

Dynamic Sales COMBUSTION is your sales manual. But do not keep it in your glove compartment. This sales diagnostics tool is divided into four powerful sections and will guide you, step-by-step, to design and maintain each component of a high-performance sales engine.

Part 1: Unbreakable MINDSET

Harness the power of *Fine-Tuned Perceptions* and rise above your challenges. Having *Upgraded Dimensions* enhances your ability to make a deeper impact with your clients. Inspire everyone around you as you operate with *High-Performance Leadership* to guide your sales vehicle to new destinations.

Part 2: Unparalleled DATA

The growth of sales professionals is determined by how they use data. Attain *Discovery Info* to increase your relevancy to your clients. *Action Info* will position you to confidently move beyond your competitors and as you utilize *Tactical Info*, you will significantly increase your referrals. As a plus, your data will become a powerful tool wrapped in *Accountability*.

Part 3: Unstoppable GEARS

Just as every piston in an engine must continue to fire, your sales engine is no different. You will *Achieve Ignition* as you enhance *prospecting* and *contacting*. You will *Create Momentum* as you elevate your skills at *presenting* and *set-up*. And you will *Develop Velocity* as you gain a new perspective of providing relevant *follow-up*.

Part 4: Unmatched STRUCTURE

Just as a building will eventually collapse without the proper structure, great sales success is reliant on strong structure. You will keep your engine running as you learn how to focus on *Your Plan* while maintaining *Your Schedule*. Most importantly, you and your team will thrive as you develop *Your Environment* and provide the opportunity to achieve transformational results.

I first created *Dynamic Sales COMBUSTION* when I began my sales journey in the financial services industry. I needed a system that was authentic and genuine to who I am. I later introduced these concepts to the media company in Southern California, creating a sales team that kept the engine running and allowed us to far exceed our expectations.

Dynamic Sales COMBUSTION is not a collection of sales theories that may work. This book is the culmination of proven strategies and techniques that I now share with businesses across the country to transform their teams, their performance, and their results.

Throughout the pages of *Dynamic Sales COMBUSTION,* you will experience energy from each *Sales Spark*, just like the one below. These tips, concepts, and insights will further enhance the performance of your sales engine.

Sales Spark:
When you fail to "drive" your sales vehicle, your sales vehicle may soon fail to drive your business.

90 DAYS

Throughout all of the books in my series, *The Think GREAT Collection*, a common theme, related to time, has been established: 90 days. We can all agree that the next 90 days are coming and none of us are strong enough to stop them. But some of us are dedicated enough to do something with them - something GREAT and something transformational.

I experienced my first transformation when I was eighteen years old. The 90 days I spent in boot camp transformed me into a United States Marine. Over thirty years ago, I learned the power of compressing actions into a 90-day period and I still use this concept today.

We all have the ability to remain laser-focused for up to 90 days, so let's use the next 90 days to create *Dynamic Sales COMBUSTION*. At the media company, we were on consecutive 90-Day Runs, unleashing our personal best for each 12-week block of time. But we did it together, as a team.

SALES DIAGNOSTIC

It is always a good idea to inspect your vehicles. To register any vehicle with the Department of Motor Vehicles (DMV), each state requires an inspection to be passed. Vehicle inspections increase the likelihood of safer vehicles on the road, fewer accidents, and greater success when driving. Failure to properly inspect your vehicle can cause unnecessary delays, increased expenses, and a miserable experience.

If you were about to embark on a long-distance road trip, perhaps lasting 90 days, you would be wise to perform an inspection of your vehicle prior to driving off. While some garages have detailed inspections, with some looking at nearly 200 specific items, some of the most common inspection points are:

- ☐ Engine Starts and Idles
- ☐ Fuel Pump Pressure
- ☐ Battery
- ☐ Fuel Gauge
- ☐ Coolant and Brake Fluid
- ☐ Brakes
- ☐ Turn Signals
- ☐ Tire Tread Depth

It certainly makes me feel more secure when I have tested all of the key areas of my vehicle before I put it in drive. In sales, you and your team will be more enthusiastic about driving your sales vehicle by completing your *Sales Inspection Checklist* (page 8), a 12-point test to check the status of your sales vehicle.

Quite often, an inspection may reveal that you only need some minor adjustments, not a major engine overhaul. Changing out a spark plug is much more cost effective than replacing your entire transmission. As a sales leader, you are best served by identifying the areas that need to be calibrated and adjusted, providing you with a reliable sales vehicle and a high-performance sales engine. Let's pull your sales vehicle up for a closer look.

Sales Inspection Checklist

Gauge the status of your sales engine before attempting your trip. Rank each, on a scale of 1-10, 10 being best.

Our sales plan is in full force	1 2 3 4 5 6 7 8 9 10
We are on track with our goals	1 2 3 4 5 6 7 8 9 10
Our next 90 days are mapped out	1 2 3 4 5 6 7 8 9 10
Teamwork occurs in all departments	1 2 3 4 5 6 7 8 9 10
We have the right sales people in place	1 2 3 4 5 6 7 8 9 10
Customer/Clients are satisfied	1 2 3 4 5 6 7 8 9 10
Prospecting - mapped out in advance	1 2 3 4 5 6 7 8 9 10
Contacting - numbers are hit	1 2 3 4 5 6 7 8 9 10
Presenting - high quality appointments	1 2 3 4 5 6 7 8 9 10
Set-Up - correct and on time (every time)	1 2 3 4 5 6 7 8 9 10
Follow-Up - relevant and consistent	1 2 3 4 5 6 7 8 9 10
Referrals - unsolicited	1 2 3 4 5 6 7 8 9 10

PART I

UNBREAKBLE MINDSET

I truly believe in positive synergy, that your positive mindset gives you a more hopeful outlook, and belief that you can do something great means you will do something great.

~ Russell Wilson

Part I

Unbreakable MINDSET

A Power Source of Unlimited Potential.

Every sale begins in our mind, but far too many sales professionals fail to harness the power of their mindset to transform their desires into results. To accomplish anything in life, we must first see it - visualize it in our minds. This is especially crucial in the world of selling, an environment that can be filled with high levels of rejection, objections, and frustrations.

The right mindset will keep you in control of two things: your thoughts and your actions. When I came up with the idea of Think GREAT, in 2008, it started by writing those two words on a napkin at a coffee shop:

Think - Control your Thoughts

GREAT - Control your Actions

As Gina's caregiver, I learned the importance of having an unbreakable mindset. It was the glue that held us together when everything seemed to be breaking apart in our lives. It allowed us to see beyond our challenges and to focus on a brighter future. It would have been easy to "mentally" toss in the towel and give up. But when things were at their darkest, our mindset shed light onto the path in front of us and kept us in motion.

Before making the decision to sell, we had the mindset that we could be successful, and we envisioned the better lifestyle that would come with a successful sales career. Perhaps the thoughts of earning additional income, paying off debt, saving for the future, and making an impact in the lives of others filled our heads. With the right mindset, the idea of selling is, dare I say it... fun?

SALES CHALLENGES

It is a lot of fun, until the challenges arrive, and arrive they will. If your mindset cracks, the circumstances you face could cause you to miss new opportunities, fail at your sales goals, or derail your entire sales career. People rarely quit selling when they are succeeding. They tend to turn off the engine when their challenges outweigh their results. But if they can overcome their challenges, great things await.

Sales Spark:
Never quit! Challenging paths often lead to unbelievable and remarkable destinations.

Regardless of how good your systems are, how talented your team is, or how sharp your sales skills are, it will be your mindset that will allow you to have the breakthroughs needed to move beyond your tough times. In addition to facing personal issues, there are hundreds of unique sales challenges that can affect your efforts and the efforts of your team. I have found that most sales professionals share the same top five.

The Top 5 Sales Challenges:

1. Time   (failure to control it)
2. Sales Skills   (stuck with old ways of doing it)
3. Systems   (slowed down by the lack of)
4. New Leads   (difficulty in generating them)
5. Perceptions   (inability to enhance them)

Despite the wide-array of unrelenting issues, many sales professionals achieve high levels of success, overcoming their circumstances and navigating through their challenges by shifting their mindset. They position themselves to be in the elite 8% category, delivering the lion's share of the sales results. How would it feel to be part of the 8% Club and have your challenges become strengths?

Sales Spark:
Don't give up! An unbreakable mindset leads to unbelievable results.

DEFINING MINDSET

The right mindset allows us to overcome the doubts, fears, and worries that stall our engines and keep us stuck in the parking lot of mediocrity. Let's take a closer look at the definition of *mindset* and how we can move ourselves and our teams closer to the opportunities directly in front of us.

> mindset
> noun
>
> - The established set of attitudes held by someone.
> - A mental attitude or inclination; a particular way of thinking.
> - A person's attitude or set of opinions about something.
> - A habitual or characteristic mental attitude that determines how you will interpret and respond to situations.

It doesn't take a rocket scientist to quickly determine that our mindset revolves around our attitudes. Possessing the right mindset gives us the power to focus and move forward, to visualize what needs to be done.

Mindsets represent our belief systems and I have found two mindsets that determine our ability to create high levels of sales combustion.

2 Types of Sales Mindsets:

1. Parked Mindset
2. Motion Mindset

They are polar opposites and you can actually feel when a person has one or the other. While people can have success with both types, the parked mindset limits the full potential of the sales "driver" and they fall short of their true potential.

Parked Mindset - In a parked mindset, you confine yourself inside of the box, rarely looking out of it. You feel that you already know all the answers, so you do not need to drive to them. People with a parked mindset rarely focus on personal development and smaller levels of rejection or disappointments can stall their vehicle. Failure is often acceptable.

Those with a parked mindset may have vast amounts of sales experience, product training, and industry knowledge. But they are limited by their belief levels. They tend to focus on the negativity of a situation rather than having a positive outlook. Those with a parked mindset often feel that they are in it alone. When they are parked, their ego is in the passenger seat.

Motion Mindset - In contrast, those with a motion mindset perceive failures and rejections as learning opportunities and grow from them. They seek out self-improvement, constantly focused on getting better. Those with a motion mindset are open to new ideas and insights. Failure is not an option.

A motion mindset allows you to focus on succeeding rather than succumbing. Those who are in motion leave their ego in the parking lot.

Sales Spark:
Your mindset must keep you in motion, so you can move beyond your challenges.

PARKED VS. MOTION MINDSET

To fully understand both mindsets, let's take a side-by-side look at some of their key characteristics. Which mindset do you consistently have? Which one describes your team members?

Parked Mindset	Motion Mindset
Status Quo	Status GROW
9-5 Mentality	24/7 Mentality
Closed to New Ideas	Open to New Ideas
Self-Serving	Team-Oriented
Fears Change	Embraces Enhancements
Negative	Positive
Points the Finger	Takes Responsibility
Ego	No Ego

It's time to get into *motion,* and to do that, we are going to rev up our engines and focus on the three key factors to developing a motion mindset that is *unbreakable.*

The Three Keys to Developing an Unbreakable MINDSET:

1. Fine-Tuned Perceptions
2. Upgraded Dimensions
3. High-Performance Leadership

CHAPTER 1

FINE-TUNED PERCEPTIONS

Adjusting Your Outlook.

There is no truth. There is only perception. At least that's how French novelist, Gustave Flaubert, saw things. I do believe there is some truth (no pun intended... I think) to what he said. After all, the truth that the earth was flat ended up being only a perception, and the notion that the sun revolves around the earth turned out to be a misguided viewpoint as well.

While I personally believe there is truth, I am also keenly aware that "perception is reality" for most people, especially when we think about sales and sales people. By possessing an unbreakable mindset, we can shift our paradigms and adjust the way we look at selling. Sales people tend to perceive selling through a distorted lens of their own experiences, but often fail to see the real truths in front of them.

Successful sales professionals fine-tune their perceptions - their awareness of the elements in their environments and their interpretation of their unique journey. Sales combustion requires us to make the necessary adjustments to our own understandings and to be open to new ways of looking at things. If we cannot, how can we expect our teams to shift their viewpoints? How can we expect clients and prospects to enhance theirs?

We can all be limited by our thoughts, remaining in the parking lot of mediocrity, instead of cruising down the road to success. By fine-tuning our perceptions, we begin to further strengthen our mindset. I believe perceptions that are left unchecked, not tuned, cause sales engines to stall. The wrong perceptions make it difficult to stay on track with our goals.

Let's take a quick look under the hood to check the current level of sales combustion you are experiencing. Score each part on a scale of 1-10, 10 being best - the highest levels of excellence.

Teamwork   Does everyone supporting sales perform as a cohesive unit?

Referrals   Are you receiving qualified referrals without asking?

Activities   Are all of your actions moving your sales vehicle forward?

Conversions   Are you converting all leads into new clients?

Knowledge   Are you gathering the info required to remain relevant?

COMBUSTION Assessment

Are You On T.R.A.C.K.?	Rank (1-10)
T Teamwork	_____
R Referrals	_____
A Activities	_____
C Conversions	_____
K Knowledge	_____

Most sales professionals and sales leaders rank themselves and their teams with a score of 25-30 from their first assessment.

Where do you rank?

0-25	Sales Engine is Idle
26-40	Sales Engine is Revving
41-50	Sales Engine is COMBUSTING

FIRST IMPRESSION

Regularly speaking in front of large groups of people, I share inspirational keynotes and conduct motivating training sessions on topics including leadership, strategic planning, and you guessed it, sales. Each audience brings a different energy level, so I naturally love groups of people who take notes, participate, and have high levels of excitement and enthusiasm.

The energy in a room filled with sales professionals is typically the most electric and lively. They are rarely shy about contributing, so I enjoy starting off by asking a question like, "Why did you choose sales?" Immediately, they shout out common responses such as, "I wanted to make more money," "I needed to control my schedule," or occasionally, the ever-honest answer, "I didn't have any other options."

But one question helps me to set the tone for fine-tuning the perceptions in the crowd. I ask, "What words come to mind when you hear Sales Person?" The answers come quickly and are rarely a surprise. But they are always unfortunate. The list of perceptions about sales people, given by sales people, are typically:

- *Pushy*
- *Annoying*
- *Pressuring*
- *Difficult*
- *Dishonest*
- *Cheesy*

I add some levity by stating, "Wow, I didn't ask for the negative ones." If their initial thought about their own role is negative, imagine how they interpret the perceptions from potential buyers. Why do most sales people think about the negative perceptions first? What is the likelihood that those thoughts will stall their sales engines? Highly likely!

Sales Spark:
The determining factor of your sales results is linked directly to the perceptions you allow as your truth.

Sales professionals tend to answer my question with their perceived truth about how buyers view sales people and some statistics may even support their thoughts. According to a survey from HubSpot Research, only 3% of people consider salespeople to be trustworthy, which is slightly higher than where politicians rank. When sales professionals allow this way of thinking to enter their minds, their *perception* of the *truth* becomes their reality and it hinders their performance. They find ways to not sell.

Nearly everyone acknowledges that negative perceptions exist of those in the sales profession, but most sales people do not feel they are the ones exhibiting those qualities. Hubspot shared another statistic that shows a disconnect from the perceptions of sellers and buyers. The study showed that only 17% of sales people view themselves as pushy, whereas 50% of buyers perceive sales people as pushy (almost three times as much).

Despite the negative perceptions of sales people, they represent the smallest minority of people in our profession. Nearly every sales person I meet is a complete opposite of the dismal stereotypes that are widely in existence. For sales combustion to occur, it is critical to have people see us the way we see ourselves.

Sales Spark:
Great sales people don't fear bad perceptions, they transform them.

After the negative perceptions are shared about sales people, by sales people, I then ask for the words that truly represent how they treat their clients and how they conduct business. I receive answers that inspire and comments that motivate and reaffirm why we chose sales. I hear descriptions like:

- *Caring*
- *Honest*
- *Knowledgeable*
- *Passionate*
- *Thoughtful*
- *Committed*

TRADITIONAL SALES FOCUS

Like most sales reps, I had the perception that receiving more training would help me to sell more. While there may be some truth to that, I discovered that training allowed me to know more but it rarely positioned me to sell more. Naturally, my fist inclination was to learn more about what I would be selling.

I attended my fair share of product training and became well-versed in annuities, mutual funds, and life insurance. Product providers delivered beneficial training, but it was more technical than tactical. I understood the products, but not the skills and techniques required to sell them. I needed "sales" training, which is far different than product training.

I attended every type of sales training you could imagine, studying techniques on prospecting, contacting, presenting, converting, closing, influencing, persuading, and the list goes on and on. There was a wide array of flavors, but nearly every version of "sales training" on the menu was devoid of the human factor. I struggled with the Traditional Way of Selling.

Traditional Way of Selling

- *SELL more products*
- *CLOSE more deals*
- *CASH bigger paychecks*

At my seminars, I can instantly determine the "way" people have been trained to sell when I ask, "How many of you want to consistently sell more products, close more deals, and cash bigger paychecks?" Hands shoot into the air, even before I can finish the question. I always ask everyone to keep their hands raised as I make the next statement.

"Keep your hands up if you like to be *sold* and *closed* when you buy something." Hands quickly lower and the final ones go down as I ask, "How would you feel if your sales rep only cared about cashing bigger paychecks?" You can usually hear a pin drop as perceptions begin to fine-tune about at the Traditional Way of Selling.

In all honesty, this is a self-centered way of looking at your business. The outcome is on the sales rep, not the buyer. Is it possible that clients will pick up on these intentions? Absolutely! This epidemic of antiquated sales training has infected nearly every business and is a major factor in the high levels of low-performing sales people.

Sales Spark:
Your outcome should always be focused on what is best for the buyer, not what is best for your wallet.

Most sales people have seen the 1992 movie, *Glengarry Glen Ross*. The film was adapted by David Mamet from his 1984 Tony-winning play of the same name. The story focuses on two days in the lives of four real estate salesmen with poor performance. They become desperate when a trainer (Alec Baldwin) is sent in to "motivate" them to sell more.

He quickly lets them know that all, but the top two salesmen will be fired, then shares his insights on selling as he forcefully states his way, "A... Always, B... Be, C... Closing." Always Be Closing. Nothing could be more unnatural, but this is not an uncommon perception of today's sales professionals. It is the traditional way of selling.

At first, this way makes sense. We think (perceive) that we need to sell, close, and cash bigger paychecks to be successful. After all, we are in sales. But as we look closer at the traditional way of selling, it is not as genuine, sincere, or positive as it could be. Would you refer a friend to someone who tried to sell and close you? I wouldn't. Would you send someone to a person who only viewed you as a paycheck? Neither would I. Luckily, there is a greater way.

THINK GREAT WAY

It is not a surprise that most people want a better way of selling. Because we all probably fell into the category of "Least Likely to Sell," we need a way that aligns with us as human beings. I have found it... STOP selling! I know what you're thinking... he has been in sales, led sales teams, written a sales book, and trains on sales. And he's telling me to stop selling? Yes!

What if you no longer had to sell, but instead you could share more solutions? What if the pressure of closing was replaced with the excitement of opening more opportunities? What if sales people no longer gave off the aura of just trying to make money, but rather, they came across as being focused on making an impact?

We deserve to operate in a way that represents how we would like to be sold to. Our clients deserve it, also. The shift in perception is simple. Stop selling; start sharing. Stop closing; start opening. Stop cashing; start delivering. Fine-tune your perception and embrace The Think GREAT Way of Selling. This is the way that empowers people to consistently take action.

Think GREAT Way of Selling

- *SHARE more solutions*
- *OPEN more opportunities*
- *DELIVER more passion*

SHARE

When we remove the pressure of selling, we can focus on one of our primary objectives - to share more solutions. Instead of setting appointments to sell, fine-tune your perceptions and share more about what you do for your clients. You will also take the pressure off of the buyer. Sharing encourages us to constantly position ourselves to provide more information that will help our existing clients and develop new clients.

It is more exciting and natural to connect with people to learn more about their exciting goals and the challenges in their path. The solutions you offer, your products and services, should help buyers to accomplish their goals and overcome their challenges. When you share solutions, you begin to create combustion and buyers will more than likely make the decision to buy... from you. You do not need to sell, to sell more.

Sales Spark:
Sharing allows you to "sell" as if your closest friend were the buyer. How would you treat your friend?

Sharing, rather than selling, allows us to create an environment in which buyers feel comfortable enough to share their goals and challenges with us. The truth is by eliminating the pressure of trying to "get" their business, you will discover the solutions they need, and you will "earn" their respect, their gratitude, and then their business.

Keys to SHARE More Solutions:

- Exude Enthusiasm
- Build Rapport
- Share Who You Are
- Identify Their Needs

Ask BETTER Questions

Sharing is the technique of asking better questions. You must master how to ask the right questions to discover their initial needs (your solutions). Unless you ask better questions that allow them to share with you, you will fail to understand the problems they need solved and you will easily begin to shift back into the selling mode.

OPEN

When we also remove the pressure of closing, we can focus on opening more opportunities. The word "Close" has so many negative perceptions attached to it. A closed door and a closed mind do not exude forward momentum. Even words like "closure" imply finality. It's over. The end. We need to shift to an open environment in our sales culture. Open the opportunity to build deeper relationships - don't close it.

By shifting to the perception of opening, sales people are empowered to connect with more people. It is more authentic to open new conversations, new ideas, and new possibilities. When we share solutions with our buyers we often need to "open up" about how our solutions have impacted us or others. The truth is when we stop focusing on closing people, opportunities will open, more than we had ever imagined... perceived.

Sales Spark:
Opening allows you to build stronger relationships and understand your clients at deeper levels.

Opening, rather than closing, allows us to build trust and develop relationships in which buyers feel comfortable enough to share more than goals and initial challenges. They begin to open up about their personal lives as well as the deeper pain points they are experiencing. By eliminating the pressure of trying to close them, you will discover how to open opportunities that were once hidden behind "closed" doors.

Keys to OPEN More Opportunities:

- Practice Active Listening
- Initiate Relevant Dialogue
- Identify Their Challenges
- Build Meaningful Connections

Ask DEEPER Questions

Opening is the strategy of asking deeper questions. You must build up high levels of mutual respect to discover a significant understanding of your clients. Unless you ask deeper questions that allow them to open up more with you, you will fail to develop meaningful relationships and you will quickly begin to shift back into the closing mode.

DELIVER

When we remove the pressure of focusing on cashing bigger paychecks, we can focus on delivering more passion. Most sales people actually do strive to deliver, but typically so they can "cash in." Fine-tune your perception so you can deliver unbridled passion, not just a presentation.

Authenticity is one of the greatest traits of a sales professional, but it is rarely used by buyers to describe their experiences. Allow your passion to lead the way, followed by professionalism, and you will not only overcome any fears associated with presenting (sharing), but you will deliver a message that is memorable, relevant, and causes action.

Sales Spark:
Delivering passion will transform your message into a pathway built on trust and understanding.

Delivering, rather than cashing, allows us to develop an unprecedented level of camaraderie with our clients; a friendship and a bond. The truth is that we can become more than just an extension of their team. We can become a valued partner that they seek out for all of their future needs.

Keys to DELIVER More Passion:

- Be Authentic
- Tell Compelling Stories
- Identify Their Goals
- Build Stronger Relationships

Ask VISIONARY Questions

Delivering is the concept of asking visionary questions. When we focus only on making money, our sales vehicle can get stuck in the present. Unless you ask visionary questions, and promote forward-thinking, you will fail to fine-tune their perceptions and you will quickly begin to shift back into the "cash bigger checks" mode.

FINAL ADJUSTMENTS

Like most people new to sales, I wanted to increase my results. So, I initially focused on improving my sales skills and increasing my knowledge of products and services. But those did not cause my sales combustion to begin. It started when I fine-tuned my own perceptions and focused on a way of selling that was natural.

When our outcomes are merely selling, closing, and cashing bigger paychecks, we do our clients - and ourselves - a tremendous disservice. Shifting to a way of sharing, opening, and delivering more passion allows our mindset and our actions to become tightly aligned. We create an environment that empowers sales people to make more calls, set more appointments, and discover more opportunities. They want to take action.

I believe in this perception so much that it is against company policy at Think GREAT for anyone to sell. So, do sales happen? Perhaps the better question to ask is, does buying happen? It absolutely does... and it happens in remarkable ways. Fine-tune your perceptions and your team's perceptions to understand the truth so they can sell The Think GREAT Way.

Now that you are making the adjustments necessary to your perceptions and you are operating in a greater way, it is time to learn how to add new dimensions to your way of selling; to add depth to your mindset.

Chapter 2

Upgraded Dimensions

What Dimension do Your Clients Experience?

It was the summer of 1983 and I was visiting the Jersey Shore with my family. We spent our days on the boardwalk, swimming in the pool, and playing in the ocean. I still remember the putt-putt golf course and Mack and Manko's Pizza as if it were yesterday. There was so much to do, but I was really excited about one item on the agenda.

One evening, my cousins and I were dropped off at the local movie theater. With my popcorn, M&Ms, and soda, I was more than ready to watch a movie, I was prepared to experience it in an entirely new way. I put my snacks down and picked up my glasses - my 3-D glasses. Placing the red and blue lenses over my eyes, I sat back and took it all in.

As the third film in the franchise, Jaws 3-D was not critically acclaimed, nor did it fare well at the box office. Ok, maybe it really wasn't that great of a movie. But it was part of a trend in the film industry, at that time, to give the viewers a new dimension in their movie watching experience. I paid close attention to every scene where the action shot off of the screen.

In 2007, Avatar easily became the biggest film at the world-wide box office. It's success once again reignited interest in 3-D films. Filmmakers wanted to give viewers a new dimension and fortunately, the old red and blue eyewear was replaced with upgraded glasses. The use of 3-dimensional films is part of the film industry's sales plan. They want to sell more tickets, and this is another option for buyers to choose from.

Most sales people fail to add any depth to the way they sell. They continue to keep using the old, antiquated methods with little to no dimension in their approach. But times have changed, and so have the expectations of buyers. They typically do not want to settle for sales professionals who lack depth.

Buying is often an emotional response, so allow your clients to experience a new dimension from you. Perhaps it is time to upgrade your sales "movie," allowing it to be experienced, not just watched.

Sales Spark:
Stop showing the same version of your sales "movie" and start projecting new dimensions to your clients.

THE DIMENSIONS OF SALES

Sales has a lot in common with math and physics. It takes a keen understanding of physics to make an engine produce combustion. Math helps us to comprehend the dimension of an object. A space or object can be informally defined by the minimum number of coordinates needed to specify any point within it. Sales people can be defined similarly.

In math, a line is considered one-dimensional because only one coordinate is required to specify a point on it. However, a square is considered two dimensional because it requires two coordinates to specify a point on it (width and height).

But then we enter a new dimension when we view the inside of a cube. This is considered three-dimensional because, as you may have already guessed, three coordinates are required to locate a point within this space.

1-Dimensional   **2-Dimensional**   **3-Dimensional**

The extent of your success is largely determined by what sales dimension your mindset is operating in. How do your clients see you? Are you 3-Dimensional? To fully understand how to add depth to our mindset, let's take a closer look at each of the three sales dimensions.

The 3 Sales Dimensions:

1–Dimensional Sales – make a buck

2–Dimensional Sales – make a living

3–Dimensional Sales – make an impact

What dimension is your mindset operating in? There is nothing wrong with wanting to make money and there is certainly no fault with striving to earn a living. Are your clients viewing you as 1–Dimensional or 2–Dimensional? What if they could experience 3–Dimensional? Are you prepared to make the shift? Many salespeople do not and some quit selling before they can make their first sale.

Operating in a 1-dimensional mindset does not allow their vehicle to move easily and can often cause their engine to blow. Roughly 90% of salespeople, who are only in it to "make a buck," are unable to make enough bucks to stay in it. There is high turnover with people functioning only with one dimension.

As some begin to consistently make more money, they seek new techniques and operate in two dimensions. They make positive enhancements in their business and in their lifestyle. Some are even asked to take on leadership roles in the hopes that their success can be duplicated in others.

But a select few operate in a unique dimension, far deeper than focusing only on commission checks and trophies. They take their sales performance to a level that impacts the lives of those around them, not just their own. 3–Dimensional Sales Leaders have a unique depth to them, which ushers in greater levels of sustainable success.

Sales Spark:
Selling is like drawing. The right technique will take a flat image and add the magic of three-dimensions.

To create that magic, let's take a closer look at each dimension and how you can add new depth to your sales efforts.

1–DIMENSIONAL SALES

Those who operate in the first dimension can have the opportunity to earn some money despite their lack of any formal sales training. They usually experience a higher level of rejection, but the occasional 'yes' is enough to keep them selling. I refer to them as 1-Dimensionsal Sales People.

Traits of a 1-Dimensional Sales Person:

- Possess an average ability to explain products and services
- Focus predominantly on their results
- Develop some new leads
- Show excitement

1–Dimensional salespeople often feel like they are running in circles to increase their results. Is this you?

2–DIMENSIONAL SALES

Those who operate in the second dimension can earn enough money to make a living. They experience fewer rejections and the occasional 'no' causes them to focus on increasing their skills. They develop referrals when they ask for them and they are often sought after to lead sales teams and achieve higher levels of team production. I refer to them as 2-Dimensional Sales Professionals.

Traits of a 2-Dimensional Sales Professional:

- Display an above average ability to teach products and services
- Focus heavily on their goals

- Develop some key clients
- Exhibit excitement and drive

2–Dimensional Sales Professionals have a high potential for earning income, but often feel like they are running on a treadmill to increase their results. They exert tremendous effort but can sometimes feel like they, and their teams, are not going where they need to. Is this you?

3–DIMENSIONAL SALES

Those who operate in the third dimension are able to make an impact in the lives around them, which in turn makes a significant difference in their own lives. They help others to thrive and they experience little to no rejection. The infrequent 'no' is perceived merely as the first two letters of 'not yet.' They often receive referrals without asking for them.

They expand upon their own goals and encourage others to pursue their dreams. More than being in a position of leadership, they tend to build dedicated teams that follow them and experience great success. Their teams also operate in unison, in the third dimension. I refer to them a 3-Dimensional Sales Leaders. People want to follow them!

Traits of a 3-Dimensional Sales Leader:

- Exhibit an unparalleled ability to share relevant solutions
- Focus heavily on their clients' goals
- Open powerful relationships
- Deliver excitement, drive, and passion

3–Dimensional Sales Leaders are in control of their thoughts, their actions, and their time. They are running on the track and moving in the right direction to accomplish their sales goals by helping their team members and clients to reach and exceed their own goals. Is this you?

Sales Spark:
Becoming 3–Dimensional does not happen by chance, it happens by choice.

BECOMING 3-DIMENSIONAL

Anyone can become 3–dimensional in sales. It does not matter how long you have been selling and is not based on how much you know. You are also not limited by age, gender, or ethnicity. While some careers, like sports, the military, or being a fire fighter require specific physical abilities, 3–dimensional selling does not rely on physical strength.

You already possess the same three components that other 3-Dimensional Sales Leaders have learned to identify and harness to help power their sales engine. Becoming a 3–Dimensional Sales Leader is about understanding these three elements and infusing their unique benefits into every aspect of your daily sales efforts.

The 3 D's of 3-Dimensional Selling:

- *Desire*
- *Determination*
- *Decisions*

Having a strong desire will help you to create a crystal–clear vision of what you need. Exhibiting a powerful determination will enhance your ability to stay on course with your goals. Making great decisions will open opportunities to create the life you dream about.

DESIRE

To succeed in sales, you must be able to distinguish between excitement and desire. While it is always good to have excitement as part of your sales presence, it takes high levels of desire to continuously operate as a 3–Dimensional Sales Leader. Most people are excited to earn more money.

But desire is much more...

DESIRE...
Must Be Deeper Than a Paycheck

By definition, a desire is something we have a strong feeling for. I encourage people to reserve their desires for more than just money. What means the most to you? Do you have the desire for a better lifestyle? Do you want to spend more time with family? Do you want to make contributions to your favorite charity or do you want to make an impact in your community? What are you passionate about? That is your desire.

Strengthening your sales efforts by focusing on your desires is like adding high-performance fuel to your engine. Most salespeople fill up their tank, push the gas pedal, and speed off in their sales efforts. But as soon as they take their eyes off of their desires, they stall. To stay in control of your sales results, stay focused on your desires - every day.

Use *The GOAL Formula* to transform your goals into realities. Successful salespeople set and accomplish sales goals, turning their desires into achievements. If your goals stay in your head, they cannot become transformational sales results. To start, write your three strongest desires, then three goals that will move you closer to achieving those desires.

My 3 Strongest Desires:

1. _____

2. _____

3. _____

3 Sales Goals that will help me to achieve my desires:

1. _____

2. _____

3. _____

Operating with strong desires eliminates the desperation exuded when you are only searching for a sale. Strong desires create a strong commitment level because desire rarely involves just one person. When you are passionate about something, it often touches the lives of the people you care most about. If you lead sales teams, encourage them to identify their desires and the goals that will allow them to succeed.

Remember, becoming 3–dimensional is about making a difference in the lives of others, not just in your own life! Most salespeople have the desire of creating financial security, developing a great lifestyle, and having more free time. Yet, I have never met anyone who aimed at these goals, only to enjoy them alone. *Activate the Power of WHO* to realize your true potential.

Sales Spark:
Transform your *desires* into the important goals that will move you closer to your greater purpose.

When you focus on strong **Desires**, you will be empowered with an unwavering **Determination**!

DETERMINATION

I made the choice to pursue a career in sales out of desperation, not preparation. When Gina was diagnosed with cancer, time was of the essence. Did I have desires? Absolutely! But at that time, my primary desire was solely focused on making sure my wife did not feel the stress of our lackluster financial situation. I needed my sales career to succeed and had the willingness to work hard to achieve this desire.

But determination is much more...

> ### DETERMINATION...
> *Must Be Stronger Than Your Challenges*

Selling is simple, but many salespeople fail because their level of determination is weaker than their circumstances. Even with a strong desire, salespeople face numerous obstacles which prevent them from staying consistent with the basic steps of selling. Sales is like walking a straight line. Most of us are capable of walking a straight line.

But what happens when we try to do it on a small boat? And what happens when that boat is tossed back and forth by waves? Although the line remains the same, staying on track becomes much more difficult when our circumstances change. A simple walk now requires a lot of determination.

Too many salespeople jump overboard as soon as their sales "boat" begins to rock a little. A powerful determination will help you overcome any waves in your path and stay on course to accomplishing your goals and achieving your desires. While selling may not always be a walk in the park, it is always a simple process.

Most great accomplishments require basic steps to be taken. Successfully selling is no different. I am sure that you have experienced difficult times during your sales journey. We have all faced seemingly insurmountable obstacles, but we only lose when we give up - when we lose determination.

 Sales Spark:
Show the strongest levels of *determination* so you can stay on track with your desires.

If you continue to sell, tough times are inevitable. Such difficulties do not last but determined 3–Dimensional Sales Leaders do. Your unwavering determination will help you to stay the course and accomplish any sales goal you set. When you exhibit an unwavering **Determination**, you will make more meaningful **Decisions**!

DECISIONS

Some research shows that we make nearly 35,000 decisions per day, with over 200 on food alone. In sales, the choices we make are like the wooden slats of a bridge, spanning across an abyss. Each decision made either builds a section of our bridge or damages a section. I was focused on taking all of the actions needed to move forward.

But decisions are much more...

DECISIONS...
Must Be Focused on Productivity

To have a 3-Dimensional mindset, I always made the decision to be there for my clients, for more than just the sale. Even though we were struggling financially, to make ends meet, I stayed unwavering on my decision, so my clients felt confident in stepping onto my bridge. I never wanted my actions skewed only by what I needed. One bad decision can destroy the trust you built with one hundred sound decisions.

Building a sturdy platform of wise and productive decisions will allow your client to confidently step across the sales bridge and choose you on the other side. While some may only take one or two steps before choosing to buy from you, others may travel the entire length of the bridge, testing each of your decisions in the process.

Today, what is the single most important decision that will be made to ensure your success? That sounds like a loaded question, but the answer means the difference between selling and failing, earning and yearning, winning and losing. The answer is simple: the most important decision will be made by your client; it is their decision to buy from you!

Developing new clients and maintaining existing ones is a never-ending journey. If you are not consciously sharing what you bring to the table, then you are subconsciously selling them about what your competition brings to the table! Your buyers will make the final decision. It is your job to consistently make smart decisions.

Each day, you will make the decision about who to call, how to follow up, when to prospect, who you should set an appointment with. Each day, some of your 35,000 decisions will be about what productive actions you need to take in order to share, open, and deliver.

Sales Spark:
Make the *decision*, each day, to take the actions necessary to help your clients to accomplish their important goals.

When we make productive **Decisions**, we will eliminate the busy work that prevents our sales vehicle from achieving the highest levels of performance. Our decisions transform us into sales leaders worth following.

CHAPTER 3

HIGH-PERFORMANCE LEADERSHIP

Sales is Always a Team Sport.

Do not skip this chapter! I know what many of you might be thinking, "I'm not a leader." I hear that all of the time from sales professionals who do not have anyone reporting directly into them and I hear it from independent contractors, like realtors, loan officers, and financial planners. Ironically, I even hear it from people managing sales teams. You may not perceive your role as a leadership role, but the truth is that every sales position is a leadership position... if you want to experience maximum performance.

In addition to going to my fair share of movies with my dad, our TV was always tuned into his favorite Westerns. If there was a John Wayne movie on, well... Pilgrim, we were watching it. My parents were huge fans of the Duke and it is no secret why my middle name is John. I even made the trek to visit his boyhood home, now a museum about his life, when I visited Winterset, Iowa. Ok, I'm a huge fan, too.

In addition to all of the old movies, we also watched every classic cowboy show on the tube, from Bonanza to the Rifleman. Although some of these were way before my time, I developed a deep fondness for them. Perhaps my favorite of the old westerns was The Lone Ranger. As the sole survivor of a group of six Texas Rangers, he fought outlaws in the Old West.

Every episode was guaranteed to have a gun fight, a horse chase, and the good guy triumphing over the bad guys. What was not to like? I can still recall the exhilarating introduction of the show, "Return with us now to those thrilling days of yesteryear." I was ready for action as the beginning of each episode continued with, "A fiery horse with the speed of light, a cloud of dust and a hearty

Hi-Yo Silver! The Lone Ranger!" To some extent, I feel that most sales people require an intro like this. Not because they save the day with their actions, but because of the mindset that keeps them stuck in the sales stables.

Many feel like they are in it alone - The Lone Ranger of Sales. While that is the perception that fills their minds, nothing could be further from the truth. I never watched an episode where the Lone Ranger succeeded by himself. Not only did Tonto save The Lone Ranger's life when the six rangers were attacked, but he saved his bacon every episode. In order for "the daring and resourceful masked rider of the plains" to lead the fight for law and order, he was part of a team.

 Sales Spark:
Sales work = Teamwork!

SALES IS A TEAM SPORT

It is unfortunate that the loyal Tonto rarely received the acknowledgements worthy of his achievements. But in sales, it is not uncommon for those who support sales efforts to rarely receive their due credit. Too many sales people rely on the efforts of a team but have the mindset that they are doing all of the work by themselves. Rarely is this the truth. A leadership mindset is needed to benefit from the power of a team.

Yes, we may make calls by ourselves, attend networking events alone, and be the sole person on an appointment, but we are always part of a team. So, what makes up our team? It can be our home office, fellow sales professionals, product providers, other departments, vendors, our supervisors and leaders, business owners, and our clients. Wait, our clients? Yes, and they can be the most valuable team player we have.

Most organizations are comprised of a wide-array of departments, ranging from Accounting and Human Resources to Operations and

Shipping. While all have their differences, every sales organization within a company is a unique entity, vastly different than any other department. It is the lifeblood of the organization and while teamwork is necessary in each department, to create combustion it is critical to have in every sales team.

The greatest sales organizations do more than operate as a group of sales professionals, they are a well-oiled machine of 3-Dimensional Sales Leaders. Although each member of the team will have their own personal objectives, they all possess an unwavering commitment to the overall good of the entire team. To benefit from being part of a team, we must first identify the differences of groups and teams.

When you walk into your work environment how does it feel? Does it feel like you are in a group or on a team? The comparison below depicts the characteristics of people in both.

GROUP	**TEAM**
• Acts as individuals	• Acts as a cohesive unit
• Focuses on personal objectives	• Focuses on common objectives
• Performs in the moment	• Performs for the future

Being a member of a group does not mean that you are a bad person or that you will not experience some success in sales. It does however, limit your full potential, especially in the eyes of your clients - your number one team member. I have been a member of both sales groups and sales teams. I will choose a team any day.

YOUR CLIENTS NEED A TEAM PLAYER

I completely understand why sales people may feel that they are in it alone. They face many of the hardest challenges by themselves. The rejections, objections, and closed doors can have a significant negative impact on their mindset. They hear all of the "No's" and the "Let me think about its" and sometimes, phones are hung up as they are talking. It can be frustrating and lonely.

Even after a phenomenal call or a dynamic presentation, we never hear back from some people. They go dark, almost as if they were the unsuspecting victims of an alien abduction. Through all these occurrences, and the dozens I did not mention, it is always in our best interest to be part of a team. Team members will help prevent our sales vehicle from running out of fuel when the odds seem to be against us. Being part of a winning team prevents us from running on fumes.

Keep Your Eyes on your Team Gauge

Most customers would rather buy from someone who is part of something bigger than their own personality, limitations, and ego. Being part of a team sends a message, to everyone you come into contact with, that you operate at the highest levels of professionalism and teamwork. Co-workers, prospects, and clients all receive your team message.

Like most other businesses, I experienced the ups and downs of the sales cycle when I worked at the media company. Not uncommon, there was a subtle wall between our sales reps and operations staff - the "Us vs. Them" mindset. But when both departments were performing like a team, our results were flawless and our clients were thrilled. Unfortunately, that was not always the case. When our Team Gauge was running on low, and we performed like a group, we often sputtered and backfired. It wasn't pretty.

As luck would have it, a unique opportunity occurred when I was working my way up the ranks. I was able to wear two hats, simultaneously, as I took over as the sales director and the operations director, leading both departments. Making the commitment to keep our fuel tanks high, I focused on empowering each person to perform as members of a team. I needed everyone to think like a leader, so they could become the best team member possible.

Without the luxury of pointing the finger at one department or the other, when a mistake was made, teamwork was our best option. I was now a team member to both departments, but to succeed, I needed both departments to operate as one. The results were unbelievable.

I developed a comprehensive sales manual, detailing our 5-step Sales System, our best practices, and our techniques and strategies for selling media services. I also designed our 7-step Operations System, along with our 6-point quality control process. Our two systems crossed over and included members of both departments in each of the transitional steps.

We grew our annual sales revenue by over 300% and nearly eliminated our mistakes, dropping from 15% to .35%. Yes, less than 1%. The key to our success was not our systems or our processes. Our success was the direct result of teamwork. We developed a team of people to think and act like leaders, even if no one reported into them. It impacted every department, not just sales and operations.

Sales Spark:
To be a team player, shift the "M" in "Me" 180 degrees and your mindset will transform to "We."

Given the choice between buying from The Lone Ranger of Sales, someone who is only a group member and in it alone, or buying from a 3-D Sales Leader, who operates as a member of a team, a cohesive unit, focused on helping buyers to achieve greater results, who would you choose? I would choose a leader, too!

Sales Spark:
Buyers want more than a product or a service; they want someone who is part of their "team."

PROMOTE LEADERSHIP

Teams do not operate at high levels of success for long without high-performance sales leaders. Possessing a strong leadership mindset is a must- have component of your sales engine. Because every sales position is a leadership position, everyone in sales must shift to a leadership mindset and identify themselves as leaders. How we identify ourselves, is a key factor to our success. There are many titles for people in the field of sales.

- *Sales Person*
- *Sales Executive*
- *Sales Manager*
- *Sales Director*
- *Sales Consultant*
- *Sales Rep*
- *Sales Agent*
- *Sales Engineer*

Some people believe that titles do not matter. They do because they provide a connection to our identity. More people in sales are striving to create titles that align with their mindset. Some sales professionals now prefer options like Director of Business Development or Director of New Business, because they don't want people to feel like they are being sold. But we all know that the new "Business" being developed is typically sales.

When I first began selling, I had no other licensed agents on my team, but I still acted like a leader and performed as a member of a team. I recognized the achievements of the departments that supported my actions, I partnered with other sales reps to support their efforts, and I focused on my clients' goals. How important is it to think like a leader?

On November 13, 1987, I earned the title of U.S. Marine. Titles are important when they have meaning. Thirty years later, I still think of myself as a Marine. Maybe I cannot run three miles in eighteen minutes and fifty seconds anymore, but it is still part of my current identity and it impacts my performance. The leadership development I received in the Corps was instrumental in my ability to achieve high-performance sales results.

Regardless of how you refer to yourself or what the current title is on your business cards, how do you think about yourself in sales? Because our performance often mirrors our self-identity, it is important to link our mindset to a title worth earning. Become a 3-Dimensional Sales Leader. If you are not thinking like a leader, then what are you thinking? If your sales team is not performing like leaders, then how are they performing?

Sales Spark:
Most sales professionals tend to perform to the level of their perceived identity about themselves. Think like a leader!

HOW DO YOU CARRY YOURSELF?

As a business coach, I have the privilege of working with businesses and business leaders, sales teams and sales leaders. I have discovered that one of the most underutilized words in the civilian sector is *bearing*. But not the definition as it relates to the direction of one point with respect to another.

More than directional, I am referring to the definition of "The manner in which one behaves or comports oneself." Bearing is one of the fourteen leadership traits of the U.S. Marine Corps. I was taught its meaning at eighteen years old and it has been a cornerstone of my sales career - my business foundation. It is defined as how you conduct yourself; how you carry yourself.

As a young Marine, even before anyone reported into me, I was expected to conduct myself, and represent my organization, with the highest levels of professionalism. Do you conduct yourself as a team player, who helps others to win? Do you carry yourself as a leader, who puts the team above your own needs? Remember, your clients are on your team. How would they describe your bearing?

Having a leadership mindset is critical because it helps us to navigate through our challenges and, sometimes, our own perceptions. It is not uncommon to hear sales people, regardless of how long they have been selling, to say that "Selling is tough." But 3-D Sales Leaders create a new version of the word "tough." We transform it into an acronym that better serves our mindset: Selling is TUF.

A Leader's Outlook on TUF:

- T   Trust You
- U   Understand You
- F   Follow You

Unless a client can trust you and understand you, they will have a tough time buying from you. As you build up high levels of both, you will position yourself to be followed. But where are you leading them? As a sales leader, you will be guiding them to their goals. Buyers would prefer to follow someone who operates confidently on a team and has the mindset of a high-performance leader!

BE TOUGHER THAN YOUR COMPETITION

Failing to stand out to buyers is a critical mistake. Just as sales professionals can find selling to be tough, many buyers can find it tough to find the right sales professional. Distinguish yourself as a 3-Dimensional Sales Leader, one who is focused on making an impact in their lives, and it will be easy for people to choose you.

Most sales professionals agree that leadership is important, but they struggle with how to start or where to begin their journey. Leadership development is critical in sales because it allows you to think and act like a leader. But it also provides three distinctive factors for us to focus on.

3 Factors of Sales Leadership:

- Lead Yourself
- Lead Your Clients
- Lead Your Team

Being committed to achieving our outcomes allows us to upgrade our engines with high-performance capabilities. But it all starts with you! When our ego gets in the way of our own development, our engines can stall, and we remain in a *status quo* environment. Things can seem stale and we tend to look at sales work as being in the grind. But when we think like a leader, we shift into *status grow*. We strive for productive actions that move our vehicle forward.

Sales Spark:
Leaders move beyond the draining zone of status quo and perform in the high-energy zone of status grow.

Lead Yourself: In my 12-month leadership development course, *The LEADERSHIP Link*, I facilitate a deep-dive, peer-to-peer discussion on each of the twelve chapters of my book, The LEADERSHIP Connection. I specifically designed a table for sales professionals, regardless of if they have direct reports, so they can transform into sales leaders.

The results have been transformational because every sales position is a leadership position. In sales, we need to think, act, and perform as leaders. By developing our leadership skills, we will do more than lead ourselves to success, we will lead our clients there, too.

Lead Your Clients: Customers have more options than ever. Most can go online to find the technical information they need. But to make tactical decisions, they need a leader to guide them. Technology is not a replacement for talent and many people who use the internet as their sales professional stand the chance of making a poor decision.

If you offer no more than the click of the mouse, you have already made the decision for your potential buyer. Leadership is what separates you from your online and live competition. When you effectively lead your clients, they will effectively lead you to more business and new referrals.

Sales Spark:
Offer more than the click of a mouse and you will go viral!

Lead Your Team: Leadership is important, even if we do not have direct reports, but it is paramount when we do. Leading sales teams can be challenging, especially if you have a group of egos. It is not easy to manage your way through strong personalities who are stuck in the status quo. But you can effectively lead them to status grow by breaking down walls, bridging gaps and connecting people in every department.

While some sales teams may be reluctant to follow you at first, consistently plant leadership seeds in them, and they will grow. Imagine how it would feel to lead a team of empowered sales leaders. It is an exhilarating feeling. It is great for you, your clients, and your team.

BE THE LEADER NEEDED

Challenging the Status Quo requires some shifts in the leader's mindset in order to do it effectively. We need to balance training and development, important tasks and priority objectives, and we need to focus on eliminating busy work while increasing productive actions. This is essential even if no one is reporting in to us.

To become the leader you need, your clients need, and your team needs, you must develop a better understanding of your role, not just your title. We can achieve balance and greater results when we enhance the perception of our role and focus on the following qualities.

3-Dimensional Sales Leader strive to...

- *Guide*
- *Consult*
- *Coach*
- *Empower*
- *Inspire*
- *Impact*

To be a 3-Dimensional Sales leader, seek out self-improvement and be open to new ideas. Fine-tune your perceptions and operate in a deeper dimension so you can consistently make an impact in the lives of others.

Now that you are forging an Unbreakable Mindset, it's time to further enhance your engine by understanding the information needed to drive in the right direction. It's time to acquire Unparalleled Data.

PART II
UNPARALLELED DATA

I want the world's data accessible. Data helps solve problems.

~ Anne Wojcicki

Part II

Unparalleled Data

Harness the Power of Information.

Each day, there was not a lot to look forward to in boot camp. But the thoughts of graduating, becoming a Marine, and seeing our families again kept our engines revving. Our days were filled with running, drill maneuvers, obstacle courses, and an array of challenging tasks. They were all designed to transform us into U.S. Marines. But there was one qualification that meant the most to the Corps - one objective that unified us all.

The eager recruits of Platoon 1095 were all looking forward to being issued our M-16A2 rifles. How critical is rifle qualification in the Marine Corps? Regardless of what job you perform, every Marine - from air traffic controllers to cooks, from pilots to recruiters - are trained, first and foremost, as a rifleman. The Rifleman's Creed sums up the level of importance.

"This is my rifle. There are many like it, but this one is mine. My rifle is my best friend. It is my life. I must master it as I must master my life." Of course, there is more to the creed, but you get the idea of its sacred importance. We were issued our weapons in the first week but would not be firing live rounds until the sixth week.

Our rifles became an extension of our bodies as we tirelessly marched with them, consistently performing precision drill movements. We also practiced taking them apart and putting them back together in record speed. Then, we attended rifle courses, studying its unique specifications and capabilities. We attained an in-depth knowledge of everything from its cycling rate to its velocity. We knew our weapons inside and out.

We were nearly halfway through boot camp before the first shot left our barrels. Why did it take so long to get us onto the firing line? Before we stepped onto the range, our leaders wanted us to have a full understanding of the rifle and the data required to course-correct our accuracy.

SALES ACCURACY

Lives are at stake if you fail to fire your weapon accurately in combat. Our drill instructors ensured that we hit the target by choice, not by chance. In sales, livelihoods are at stake when we fail to accurately hit our goals. Too many sales people rush into the field without understanding sales and the data required to consistently course-correct their accuracy.

While some sales leaders suffer from too little, I see more who are overwhelmed with too much. It is not a surprise when we consider that the newest unit of data measurement is the zettabyte, a unit of information equal to one trillion gigabytes, or 1,000,000,000,000,000,000,000 bytes. So, is technology a blessing or a curse? Perhaps it is a combination of both.

We have an abundance of information we can use to research, review, and guide our sales efforts. But quite simply, sales data must cause one thing: productive action. If action is not your outcome, then the question must be asked, "What are you using the information for?" Below is a list of some common data points that can be tracked and used to improve results.

- *Revenue*
- *Research*
- *Trends*
- *Calls*
- *1ˢᵗ Appointments*
- *Proposals/Quotes*
- *Order Status*
- *Referrals*
- *Profit Margins*
- *Follow-Up*
- *Opportunities*
- *New Clients*
- *Events*
- *Opportunities*
- *Conversion Ratios*
- *Revenue/Profits*

Without question, there is an unlimited amount of information we could use, but what data should we use? It is essential to prioritize and utilize the information required to take action. But many sales professionals suffer from data overload and experience problems with their sales engine.

Sales Spark:
Sales leaders can often experience an "Engine Misfire" between the data collected, and their actions taken.

Putting together reports, lists, analytics, graphs, charts, and plans can cut into our day. So, I have simplified sales data into two types that help our engines to achieve top performance: In and On.

IN   Important DATA   - Keeps our sales engine RUNNING

ON   Priority DATA   - Keeps our sales vehicle ON TRACK

Both types of data are necessary, so we need to ensure that the data collected is unparalleled. It must be superior to the data discovered and used by our competition. So, let's take a closer look at the definition of *unparalleled* so we can course-correct our way to success.

Un•par•al•leled
adjective
- Having no parallel or equal.
- Exceptional.
- Unique in kind or quality.

While data is critical, it can be damaging if not balanced properly. Most statistics show that the average time sales people spend selling is about 22% of their day. So, where does the other 78% go? There are many actions that significantly minimize our effectiveness and the number one culprit of lost selling time typically involves the misuse of data.

Three Areas where Sales People Dedicate Too Much Time:

1. Compiling/Reporting Data
2. Handling Customer Service/Support
3. Attending Unnecessary Internal Meetings

SALES HARVEST

Sales data can be used for several relevant objectives, including how to identify new buying trends. It also helps us to forecast, make projections, prepare budgets, and is valuable for deciding on upcoming purchases and expansions. But the unquestionable main purpose of data is to course- correct. Data allows us to hit the target (goals) consistently.

Most sales people dream of the big harvest, driving their sales tractor and reaping the rewards of their hard work. But they often find themselves stuck in the sales weeds when they are unable to get their pistons firing in sync with their data. Unparalleled data serves three functions.

3 Functions of Unparalleled Data:

1. Connects to Goals
2. Supports Course-Correction
3. Measures Success

Is your data allowing you to set and accomplish your goals? Are you using it to course-correct your performance and the actions of your team? Are you tapping into your data to set benchmarks and measure your success? Most importantly, is your data unparalleled?

KEEPING TRACK OF IT ALL

I know what you might be thinking. Not only is there a ton of data I could use, but how do I keep track of it all? Sales leaders embrace accountability as a powerful tool for self-growth. As young recruits, we were issued more than just a rifle in boot camp. We were also issued the *U.S. Marine Corps Rifle Marksmanship and Data Book.* Data was vital to our success.

Our goal was to qualify with our weapon and move to the next phase of recruit training. We left nothing to chance and tracked every shot fired. Using it to do more than just take notes, we reviewed it with our drill instructors, for the sole reason of making constant improvements.

Before we fired our first shot, we knew the unparalleled data we would need to collect, analyze and use to course-correct our performance. The Marines sum it up best when describing their Data Book:

> *Of all the available tools that assist the shooter in firing accurately and consistently, the data book, if properly utilized, is his most valuable asset.*

When properly utilized, in unison with an unbreakable mindset, your data will be your most valuable asset. Imagine hitting the target and accomplishing your goals by choice, not by chance. The next three chapters will teach you the three keys to acquiring the data you need, and the accountability required to wrap it all up into a powerful tool for combustion.

The Three Keys to Acquiring Unparalleled DATA:

1. **D**iscovery Info
2. **A**ction Info
3. **T**racking Info

> **A**ccountability

Chapter 4

Discovery Info

Understanding Your Clients.

How would you feel if you walked into your doctor's office and you were prescribed medication before being asked any questions? What if an operation was recommended before they even took your vitals? Like me, you would probably run for the door and start looking for a new doctor. That is exactly how buyers feel when a sales diagnosis is made before the right questions are asked. The final prognosis: trust deteriorates.

How important is trust in a doctor-patient relationship? In my home, it is paramount, considering that my wife had four bouts with cancer, suffered cardiac arrest, and now has a weaker heart than most people. But an article in Physicians Weekly, suggests that many doctors are losing ground in the arena of patient trust. Dr. Linda Girgis' article, *Why Doctors Are Losing the Public's Trust*, states, "They see us as driven for profit."

She goes on to say that patients "feel we don't listen to their concerns anymore and don't care what they want or need. The public is losing their trust in us." She continues to share that "There has been an erosion in this relationship over recent years. Doctors are no longer held in such high esteem as they were decades ago."

The survey from HubSpot (page 19), which showed only 3% of buyers trust sales people, also shared that doctors typically are at the top of the trust factor. It may not be a surprise that politicians firmly hold onto the bottom level, but it is concerning that patients are losing trust in their doctors. Many prescribe before they ask.

According to Dr. Girgis, many patients feel doctors are no longer listening to them, and a lack of eye-to-eye contact is a sign that doctors are more interested in the patient's digital record than them. It becomes an indication that "we are pushing them through... and don't care about them." Is it possible that buyers may feel the same way about sales people?

Dr. Girgis' solution to building patient trust levels up is simple: "Our profession needs to re-establish integrity." Perhaps we should apply this to sales. If trust is lessening with doctors, it can more easily happen in sales. Relationships can rapidly dissolve when we fail to connect with people and discover the information needed to offer relevant solutions.

Sales Spark:
Recommending any action, prior to acquiring the proper data, sends up a red flag to buyers.

When we meet with prospects or even existing clients, we should always be looking to increase our knowledge about them and their circumstances. Every person, every relationship, and every conversation is different. We need to search for the data that allows us to have a deeper understanding of our clients, our competition, and the steps we are recommending.

Acquiring the right D.A.T.A. builds high levels of trust. Each piece of information leads to a deeper understanding of our clients, our rivals, and our solutions. When we wrap it all up with accountability, it becomes unparalleled data, and prevents us from making a diagnosis too quickly.

- **D** Discovery Info ⇨ Understand Clients
- **A** Action Info ⇨ Understand Rivals
- **T** Tactical Info ⇨ Understand Solutions
- **A** Accountability Wraps it all together

INTEGRITY IS MORE IMPORTANT THAN COMMISSION

Nowadays, every patient has more access to medical knowledge online than ever before. But they still require personal attention to build trust, perhaps more now than ever. The same thing can be said of our buyers. When sales professionals make a diagnosis before they learn about the buyer's real needs, it speaks volumes about their intentions and character.

As a licensed financial services representative, I primarily sold insurance and mutual funds, and combinations of both. Our "flagship" product was the VUL (Variable Universal Life) policy, which provided life insurance coverage and a cash account that could be invested into different products, including mutual funds. Like any product, there are pros and cons.

But far too often, I heard many sales reps describe only one specific pro - the commission. Even if the client only made monthly premium payments, the VUL paid out handsomely, based on the annual premiums. We offered other products, like term insurance, which also had pros and cons. But it had a significantly lower payout to the salesperson.

While I am not intending to create a debate about term insurance and permanent insurance, it is a glaring example of the "predetermined diagnosis" that exists in sales. Many of my colleagues already knew what they would be selling, before the appointment even began. Some brought the product application with them, as if they had already "closed" the deal; made the prescription.

They knew exactly what direction they were going to guide the client, whether the VUL was the right solution or not. It is easy to guide people to the place you need them to go, so you can "cash bigger paychecks."

 Sales Spark:
Avoid having a Predetermined Sales Diagnosis when meeting with buyers.

I was an expert at preparing Top Ramen for a reason. It was not because I failed to sell. It was because term insurance commissions did not always provide the income required to live high on the hog.

But I was able to look myself in the mirror each night, knowing that I provided the right solutions, based on my discovery information.

Great sales leaders ask questions to discover the information needed to fully understand the client and best serve their needs. The right questions provide us the knowledge to guide buyers to the place they need to be.

THE POWER OF KNOWLEDGE

I have never liked the perception that sales is a numbers game, where the strategy is to throw as much as you can against the wall to see what sticks. People do not want to feel like they are just a number - a dollar sign for their salesperson. Sales should never be only about the numbers. Sales is a knowledge game, where the strategy is to understand your clients, so you can prescribe the right solutions.

While sales is a game of knowledge, I first want to challenge the misconception that "Knowledge is Power." Searching only for knowledge has led to sub-par, poorly-timed questions that fill space during a presentation. "What will it take to earn your business?" may seem like a reasonable question to ask. But as we develop deeper relationships, clients tend to naturally share that information. Knowledge alone does not equal power.

Knowledge ≠ Power

I have never seen knowledge convert into energy that can move our sales vehicles. Combustion, however, occurs when we attain more than random information. We must focus on gathering the discovery information required to better understand our clients and guide them to take action. I have found an equation to achieve more than power for your sales engine.

Knowledge + Action = Combustion

We'll cover *Action Info*, more in Chapter 5.

STOP LOSING CLIENTS

One huge mistake that many salespeople often make, when meeting with prospects and clients, is talking more than listening. Wanting to sound like an expert, they typically state facts to let the buyer know how much they know. They give more information than they receive, and this lack of confidence may cause many in sales to fill gaps of silence with "impressive" dialogue yet fail to gather necessary data.

Sales Spark:
You cannot play the Knowledge Game by only talking. You need to ask the questions that "move" people.

It takes a confident sales leader to ask the right questions and guide the conversation in the direction that best serves the client. But what questions are the best to ask? They are any question that provides the *Discovery Info* needed to share your solutions. A search online will pull up hundreds of the "Best" sales questions. Of course, best is a relative term.

Common Sales Questions:

What is your budget?
Are you happy with your current vendor?
What level of service are you looking for?
Are you the decision maker?
How soon can we begin?

But you do not want to be the common salesperson, do you? As sales leaders, we are in the knowledge business. We need to ask "better" questions, so we can share more solutions.

Most sales people overthink the process of gathering data and fail to even gain the basic information required to move people forward. Think of your next client appointment the same way you do when you visit your doctor. They have a process for making us feel more comfortable and opening up about what's going on with our bodies. Nurses typically start your visit by gathering the following information.

Blood Pressure: 120/80
Heart Rate: 70 bpm
Body Temp: 98.6

This basic information serves a purpose. It allows them to understand us and identify any immediate needs. Once they have this data, doctors begin to ask deeper questions like, what brings you in today? How are you feeling? What symptoms do you have? A good doctor understands the patient and asks questions to help guide the discussion. To excel in the knowledge business, we must master the art of asking questions. Ask more!

A.S.K.

Always Seek Knowledge

Great sales questions move us beyond the basic information needed to "close" a sale and open the door to their goals and challenges; they unlock the deeper knowledge needed to make an impact.

FACT-FINDER

Because the right information allows us to identify needs and successfully guide our customers through the sales process, salespeople consistently cite data as being critical for client strategy. But I have found that most use a notepad, at best, to capture the information required to make a significant impact.

How would you feel if your doctor tried to memorize everything you were telling her or she just jotted notes on a random piece of paper? What if she never looked at your records... the collection of your vital data? What message would this send to you? Perhaps it would let you know that you are not important.

The use of professional data forms build trust. Regardless of if I was selling financial services, media services, or professional development services, I have always used a simple, non-threatening form with our company logo at the top and my best questions. I still use one today.

A Fact-Finder not only allows me to collect information, but it sends a message to my clients. Using a professional form lets them know that I am not winging it. I am taking the data shared with me seriously. Using a Fact-Finder conveys a feeling that I will be doing something with their information. Not merely gaining knowledge but attaining it to take action.

UNDERSTAND YOUR QUESTIONS

So many people ask me, "What is the best question you use?" It's as if they believe there is one magic question that causes the stars to align and open the floodgates of new business and endless referrals. I have not found that question, nor am I looking for that mythical creature. I have found, however, two key factors of each question I ask.

The Two Key Factors of Each Question:

1. Knowledge   - Do I understand my question?
2. Action   - Do I know the best time to ask my question?

While your Fact-Finder contains your key questions, you must do more than just know what is on your form. Merely reading questions off of your Fact-Finder is impersonal and awkward. In addition to memorizing our most important questions so we can integrate them into any conversation, we must understand the deeper meaning of each one.

It is not just the questions we ask that guides every conversation, it is the answers we discover that allows us to take each next step with our clients. A Fact-Finder is best used when you know each question and the question after it, so they flow together seamlessly to expand your knowledge of the buyer and understand the actions needed.

In addition to exhibiting the highest levels of integrity when asking questions, we need to have a genuine interest in their answers. While asking the right question is crucial, it must be asked at the right time. Asking the right question at the wrong time may cause your sales vehicle to inadvertently hit the brakes and lose momentum.

Imagine how a buyer would feel if, during our discussion, they let me know that one of their family members was recently hospitalized and I looked at my Fact-Finder and replied, "I'm so sorry to hear that. What would it take to earn your business?" The question may be the right thing to ask, but the timing is way off.

Sales Spark:
How you ask your questions is a key indicator to buyers of how you will handle their needs.

It is easy to have sales appointments get off course as relationships are built and other topics are discussed. Everything from kids and sports to the economy and weekend plans can affect the direction of your sales vehicle. Your Fact-Finder helps keep you on track with gathering data as you build relationships. Leaving a client session without all of the info required to take action is frustrating for both parties. But it sends a message, loudly and clearly to your buyer - you do not care.

THE ART OF ASKING

Now, it is time to ask the questions that will provide the data to understand our buyers and share the solutions that will make an impact. We already know that failing to ask the right questions will cause a major disconnect.

Sales Spark:
Do not ask questions so you can sell more; ask questions so you can know more.

Acquiring discovery information is a journey, not a race. You cannot rifle through your questions and expect to build trust. Buyers prefer to know where you are going with your questions. If they do not understand where you are guiding them, they may suspect that they are being manipulated. Do they feel you are there to collect only a paycheck or to collect the knowledge that will help them?

Sales Spark:
To build trust, your client must understand that you are focused more on the person than the profit.

Disappointing experiences are all too common on sales appointments and the lack of well-timed questions makes the majority of client relationships shorter lived than a Hollywood marriage! There is an art to asking questions and it is in your best interest to become a world-class artist. Focus on three techniques to ensure that your sales brush glides across the canvas authentically and with integrity. Your questions will allow you to create a masterpiece.

3 Techniques to Acquire Discovery Data:
1. Interview People
2. Identify Needs
3. Uncover Challenges

Interview People

When the focus is selling and closing, sales appointments can feel more like an interrogation, where the sales person leads buyers to the answer they want to hear. To share more solutions and open more opportunities, treat each client meeting like an interview. Get to know the person.

If we expect meaningful answers, we must ask meaningful questions. While I never ask permission to ask questions, I do ask permission to take notes... on my Fact-Finder. As I guide the questions into deeper discussions, I want to show that I am listening and fully in the moment.

I prefer to start with open-ended questions that provide a wide stroke of the brush like, "How long have you worked at XYZ Company?" or "What made you choose XYZ Company?" Starter questions like these can put people at ease because they open the door for nearly any type of answer. Strong starter questions will create a tidal wave of dialogue.

Identify Needs

As the interview continues, I build on our discussion and guide the conversation to what they do by asking, "Would you tell me a bit more about your role?" Studies show that most people prefer to talk about themselves, so I let them. Remember, you are their consultant and the questions you are planting need to yield a harvest of quality information.

As rapport builds, guide the conversation and ask questions about any goals they are working on, any new projects and initiatives, or any new products, services, and offerings they will have.

Uncover Challenges

It is exciting to talk about goals because they provide hope and inspiration. But they also come with challenges. During my interview, I am ultimately looking for buyers to share their challenges with me; to let me know the areas I can fix with one of my solutions.

Because most people do not start out a conversation with their challenges, I connect my questions in an exploratory way, allowing them to comfortably share more information with me.

As rapport continues to develop, better questions like, "What are your biggest challenges?" or "What roadblocks do you face?" are usually enough to start a deeper level of dialogue and allow me to see their pain points - the areas that will need a prescription or an operation.

To discover the information needed to support your clients, ask your questions in a logical order by keeping your intentions clear and building trust along the way.

Starter Questions ➡ **Goal Questions** ➡ **Challenge Questions**

Sales people often stand in their own way by asking the wrong questions or not asking enough questions. Having a deeper understanding of the data you need to course-correct your actions is crucial. Every industry is different, so it is up to you to identify the questions that yield the best data and add those to your Fact-Finder.

By adding high levels of integrity into your process and mastering the art of gathering discovery information, you have moved out of your own way, leaving only one other person blocking your path to developing new clients - your competition. To move beyond your rivals, you will need to gather additional data.

CHAPTER 5

ACTION INFO

Staying Ahead of Your Competition.

Do you stand out? Are you unique? Most sales people readily agree that they are the best option for their clients, the star player of the game. In the highly competitive world of sales, the solutions we provide to customers must be better than the solutions our competitors provide them. If a buyer were to pick someone to be an extension of their team, should they choose you?

There are hundreds of professional sports franchises throughout the world, playing in stadiums and arenas packed with screaming fans who cheer for their home teams and star athletes. At restaurants and sports bars, big screen televisions are surrounded by people wearing team jerseys, hats and shirts, all cheering at the top of their lungs. They pay top dollar for great seats, merchandise and memorabilia.

But what is the primary focus of any professional sports team? You may think that winning is their main objective. But that is only one step toward their primary goal: selling. They sell tickets, merchandise, advertisements, and TV/radio rights. The bottom line: winning teams sell more! And teams win more by knowing those who they play against.

Today, nearly 25 professional sports teams worldwide are valued at over one billion dollars. Leading the pack is Manchester United, a British soccer team valued at $1.8 billion. In football, the Dallas Cowboys are valued at $1.6 billion, and in baseball, the New York Yankees are valued at $1.3 billion. In golf, Tiger Woods has a personal net worth that is estimated at over a half billion dollars. Four different sports that all share one common strategy: obtain an in-depth knowledge of your rivals.

Before a game, athletes often watch video clips of their upcoming opponents. After losing a game, you can rest assured that the coach will be playing back footage, analyzing their competition, and making the necessary adjustments. Winning is not necessarily about playing better, it is about outplaying your rivals. Unfortunately, most sales people know very little about the people striving to beat them.

Sales Spark:
Know more about your competition so you can outplay them and win more opportunities.

YOUR RIVALS

Put in its most simplistic terms, our prospects are someone else's clients and our clients are someone else's prospects. In sales, we cannot expect to win if we are not willing to develop a deep understanding of our competition. But some sales people have the mindset that they do not have competition.

Unless you have a revolutionary item on the market, you have competition. Even if your product or service is so new that no one has anything like it, you will not have that advantage for long. Like children pulling the blankets over their heads, in hopes the boogey man won't find them, many sales people think, "If I don't talk about them, they will go away - they are not really there."

Here's the difference: the boogey man goes away when you turn on the lights. Your competition does not. We must flip the switch and illuminate the pathway to victory, for us and for our clients. The first step is to acknowledge that we have competitors, people who are trying to pass us up and be the first to cross the finish line.

To win, we cannot stay on the sidelines. We must get in the driver's seat. So, let's take a closer look at the definition of *rival* so we can identify who we are playing against.

ri•val
noun

- A person competing with another for the same objective or for superiority in the same field of activity.
- One striving for competitive advantage.
- To attempt to equal or surpass.

Is there someone out there competing for superiority within your sales game? Is there someone striving for the competitive advantage against you? Is there someone attempting to surpass you? You bet there is! You are someone else's rival and you must drive like the race is at stake.

Understanding our competition is not an option; it is an obligation of every sales "athlete." We must always assume that our rivals are researching us and trying to find out why our clients decide to drive with us. Your competition is researching ways to take the actions necessary to lure your clients away from you. If you truly believe you are different than your competition, do you have the data to prove it?

COMPETITIVE DATA

Being a salesperson is a lot like being an athlete. In sales, too, there is a great deal of competition, occasional screaming and cheering, and usually some shiny trophies. But to be a champion you must be able to anticipate the moves of your opponent. After all, the best offense is a good defense. You cannot defend against someone you know little about.

Only knowing the rules and regulations of your sales game is never enough to win. You may be the best player the game has ever seen, but if you lack the information needed to know your rivals, you may lose more races than you had anticipated. To drive as a 3–Dimensional Sales Leader, you must have an intimate knowledge of your competition – the people who are trying to drive away with your clients and your sales.

Sales Spark:
When you play all out, you are not the only one who wins. So does your client.

How well do you know your rivals? I am not only referring to the company they work for and the products and services they sell, I am talking about the information that changes your sales game and gives you the 'home court' advantage. Most sales people do not fully understand what differentiates them because they fail to research their rivals. Without the right data, our sales engines may fail to drive us to the winner's circle.

When it comes to winning new clients, there is no second place in sales. If your competition's horsepower is greater than yours, you may watch your client buckle up in the sales vehicle just ahead of yours. It is in your best interest to know how your competition operates and there are many ways to research them.

You can visit their websites and take a close look at their testimonials. Of course, no one posts anything bad said about them, but it will give you an idea of the positive attributes people are saying. You can follow them through social media and you can also find online reviews that will say the good, the bad, and the ugly.

It is highly unlikely that your rivals will voluntarily provide you with a detailed list of weaknesses that you can use to your advantage, but you can find out why people chose them or chose someone else. The number one source of meaningful, game-changing data about your rivals comes from your buyers. Whenever you meet with a client or a prospect, never gloss over the data they possess that will allow your engine to create more combustion.

RIVAL ASSESSMENT

To gain a better understanding of our competitions' strengths and weaknesses, let's pop the hood again and take a quick look at the competitive data we need to gauge their performance, so we can increase ours.

The P-5 Rival Assessment allows us to look at five key categories to understand the impact our rivals are making on the people we want to sell to. Score each part on a scale of 1-10, 10 being best. If they have high-quality "Products" that exceed the expectations of a buyer, you may want to rank them around a 9 or a 10. If their "Pricing" is not on point, and perceived as too high by most buyers, you may want to rank them as a 6 or a 7.

Products Do they offer the highest quality, full range of products and services?

Pricing Is their pricing on par with buyer expectations? Is it competitive?

People Does their team consistently deliver the ultimate customer experience?

Positioning How strong is their market reputation?

Pact How strong is their bond with your prospect? Do they have a deep relationship already established?

P-5 RIVAL Assessment

How do they Perform?	Rank (1-10)
1 Products	_____
2 Pricing	_____
3 People	_____
4 Positioning	_____
5 Pact	_____

According to an article by Intandemly.com, "Every business, before choosing a vendor, evaluates at least 4- 6 companies on an average." So, buyers already possess the data you need. You just need to start asking them for it so you will better understand your competition. Is it possible for your rivals to have a different score with two different buyers? Absolutely!

While a lower score may equal less resistance, a higher score does not mean that you are out of the race. It just means that you need higher performance in your sales engine. Consistently evaluating your rivals will allow you to gauge the enhancements you need to make to ensure that you are able to make an impact on The Relationship Wave.

RIDE THE WAVE

As the vice president of the media company, I worked closely with my sales team to develop a deep knowledge of our competitors. We knew that our prospects were typically using Point 360 or Lightning Media. Both companies were larger than us and had much deeper pockets. They could throw money at any situation.

We did not have that luxury, so we relied on our knowledge of what they did well and where they dropped the ball. We knew all about their products and services, their turn times, and their full capabilities. But I always sought out the deeper knowledge of what my clients and prospects experienced with them.

A couple of years after I started working at the media company, I was reconnected with a friend from the film school at USC. David was now an editor for Comedy Central's number one show, South Park. I visited their studios and had a tour of their entire operation. It was amazing. I also had the opportunity to meet Frank, their supervising producer, and learn more about his role and who they were using for deliverables.

It was a great meeting and it seemed like we hit it off. Frank is a straight shooter and let me know that they had a reliable vendor and were probably not going to "try and fix it if it's not broken." I respected his thoughts, but I knew that this vendor did not have the team that I had. At some point, they would drop the ball. But for now, South Park was at a high point on the Relationship Wave with my rival.

Below is a graph of the Relationship Wave, an illustration I use to show the status of the client–rival relationship. I have found that most vendor-buyer relationships have ups and downs. Although it is challenging to develop a new client when their relationship with their salesperson is on the High Point of the wave, it is almost certain that you will win them over when the relationship falls to the Low Point.

High Point = possible score of 50 with the P-5 Rival Assessment.

The Relationship Wave:

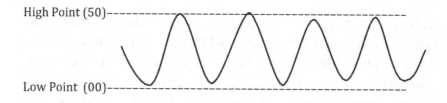

So, did South Park's vendor eventually drop the ball? They did! Although it took about two years, the opportunity opened when the Relationship Wave hit the Low Point. When I received the call from Frank, I moved onto the Relationship Wave and focused my efforts at staying at a High Point.

By asking the right questions and building a deeper relationship, I was able to keep a close eye on the Rival Assessment score of my rival, not only with South Park, but with the hundreds of other clients we serviced. How many of your potential clients are at the bottom of their Relationship Wave with their salesperson (your competition)?

Sales Spark:
Ask the necessary questions so you always remain at the High Point of the Relationship Wave.

EXPAND YOUR FACT-FINDER

"My clients love me," is a common response from sales people when I ask about their competition. Ignorance may be bliss, but it takes you out of the driver's seat when dealing with your competition. To avoid this disadvantage, we must expand our fact-finders with deeper questions, specifically about our rivals. When we stop ignoring our competitors, we can begin to gather the *Action Info* needed to stay ahead of them.

We need the hard facts, the gems, and the undeniable evidence that will influence people to choose us. The success of your sales vehicle is largely based on your ability to attain the deeper answers about your competition, so you can properly score them on the P-5 Rival Assessment. Remember, your clients and prospects already have the answers you need.

It is in our best interest to have deeper dialogue with our buyers, According to the article, *10 Tips on How to Research Your Competition*, published by Inc.com, "When it comes to identifying sources of information about your competition, don't skip over the obvious ones—like your customers. Speaking to customers is one of the best (and cheapest) ways of gathering factual information on competitors."

I ask five key competitive questions, in a sequential order, as the relationship is developing with buyers. By enhancing your fact–finder with these questions, you will discover the answers on how to win more clients and you will send a message to your buyer - you care enough to ask.

5 Competitive Questions:

1. Who do you currently buy from/use?
2. How long have you been working with your current rep?
3. What do you like best about him/her?
4. What is the number one reason you stay with him/her?
5. If you could design the perfect client-vendor relationship, how would it be different?

Questions 1-3 are starter questions to allow you to begin the meaningful dialogue about your competition. Question number 4 goes a bit deeper and explores the main reason the buyer has made the decision to choose your rival. I discovered that South Park's number one reason for staying was turn times. Their vendor was able to deliver on that one critical aspect.

I knew that we could do it, too. But I at least understood their hot button. I have found that many clients are with their competitor because they do one thing very well, even though there are other parts of the puzzle that do not fit as well. Hence, question number 5 allows them to tell me their description of a "High Point" relationship. That is the answer I strive for.

The only way to find out why your buyers choose your rivals is to ask. But most salespeople, who feel uncomfortable asking these questions, are typically focused only on making a sale or closing a deal. When the buyer is not threatened by a "close," they will open up more about your rivals and you can guide them through the questions. I am merely sharing information, so the questions flow smoothly, naturally.

Sales Spark:
Position your clients to share the data that will make the biggest impact in their decision-making process.

In a world of similar offerings, it is imperative to stand out. As we collect the data needed to speed ahead of our rivals, remember, it is the experience and integrity we bring to the table that truly distinguishes us from our rivals. Now that we know more about our competition, do our buyers know what makes us stand out? What makes us unique?

What differentiates you?

_____

_____

_____

TAKING ACTION

Now that we have started to gather the data that will allow us to evaluate our rivals, there is only one thing to do with it: take action. Understanding your competition builds confidence and allows you to communicate more effectively with your target clients. But what actions can we take, and track, to increase the performance of our sales engines?

The knowledge we acquire moves us to focus on three critical actions: our performance; our results; our enhancements. We need to achieve higher performance in all three. Knowledge applied to your Action Data will lead to greater results.

Action Data:

1. Performance
2. Results
3. Enhancements

Performance:

Increase the quality of our calls, appointments, tours, proposals.

Results:

Increase the accuracy of our new business, new clients, profit margins.

Enhancements:

Increase the effectiveness of our training, development, and retention.

Sales Spark:
Sales champions develop a deep understanding about their competition.

Competitors are like obstacles on the road. Without the right data, you will either hit the brakes and stop, swerve off the road and end up in a ditch, or you will run into them and cause a pile-up.

When you have an intimate knowledge of how they drive their sales vehicles, you will not only increase the horsepower of your engine, but you will enhance your driving skills and ensure that you out-maneuver them.

CHAPTER 6

TACTICAL INFO

Making a Strategic Diagnosis.

So, your nurse has taken your vitals and your doctor has visited with you, examined the x-rays, and reviewed your charts. No matter how much you like him and his team, your relationship is most likely based on a single question. Does he make the right recommendations for your health? You could have gone to his competition, but you chose your doctor for one reason. You buy what he sells: his solutions.

Even though the medical field currently has some of the highest levels of trust, is it possible that doctors make incorrect recommendations to their patients? According to an article from NCBI (National Center for Biotechnology Information), "It is believed that preventable medication errors impact more than 7 million patients and cost almost $21 billion annually across all care settings." How is this possible?

The article adds, "About 30% of hospitalized patients have at least one discrepancy on discharge medication reconciliation." That is a lot more tactical errors than I wanted to hear regarding the medical profession. If some doctors are falling short on their recommendations, how likely is it that this is happening with sales professionals?

But medical errors do not stop with just prescriptions. The article, *Surgery mix-ups surprisingly common*, from Health.com states that "Catastrophic surgical errors are a lot more common than the public thinks." In the article, *Thousands of Mistakes Made in Surgery Every Year,* published on WebMD, "More than 4,000 preventable mistakes occur in surgery every year at a cost of more than $1.3 billion in medical malpractice payouts."

But wait, aren't doctors highly trained and educated? To become a medical doctor, you are required to graduate from college, pass the MCAT, and then complete medical school, followed by 3-7 years in a residency program. Their licenses are earned at the completion of medical school. It makes little sense that so many patients can be impacted poorly from medical professionals who are so highly qualified.

If this is happening with doctors, how many buyers are negatively impacted by their sales people? Of course, there must also be high standards regarding the ability to make sales recommendations, right? While some sales people may possess a license (real estate, life insurance, etc.), which can all be attained infinitely easier than a medical license, others may only hold a certification. But the clear majority of sales people only have one qualification, their titles: Sales Associate, Sales Manager, VP of Sales, etc.

The undeniable impact of sub-par recommendations to clients is an epidemic in sales. Because the focus is, "Sell more, close more, and cash bigger paychecks," it is easy to see why most buyers are uneasy and have reservations about what is being prescribed to them. It also explains why the trust factor is so low in sales. Ultimately, people choose you, just as they choose their doctors, for one thing: what you are recommending.

 Sales Spark:
Understand your clients so you can always make the recommendations that deliver a positive impact.

BUYER'S REMORSE

We have all been there. We are out looking at a new car, a TV, or perhaps a propane BBQ grill with a combo smoker and charcoal grill. They may be a bit expensive, but right now they are on sale. We weigh the options until a helpful sales person steps up and shares all of the bells and whistles. You need it right now. Done!

Sold! And then you get home and do some thinking. Do I really need this? Can I truly afford it? Was it really a good deal?

We have all experienced buyer's remorse and it happens more than we may think. In real estate, according to a Trulia survey, "44 percent of Americans have regrets about their current home or the process they went through when choosing it." In the automotive world, according to an article on AARP.org, "At least 50 percent of people who lease cars experience buyer's remorse at some point during the contract."

Whether buying a home or a car, a sales person is typically assisting. So, why is there such a high rate of anxiety and regret after many sales? The sales person is not digging deep enough to gather the data that will eliminate buyer's remorse, a phenomenon we experience that is generally associated with the psychological theory of cognitive dissonance. It is so wide-spread that studies have been conducted to understand it better.

Sales Spark:
Great sales leaders understand the questions that cause buyer's remorse - before they are even asked.

To detail buyer's remorse, a scale was created by Sweeney, Hausknecht, and Soutar, which identified three elements (one emotional, two cognitive) of this phenomenon. The emotional element pertains to how we feel about our purchase. What emotions did we experience? The first cognitive element focuses on the wisdom of our purchase. Did we make the right decision?

But it is the second cognitive element that points to the salesperson. The "Concern Over the Deal" component acknowledges a major factor that significantly impacts our buyer's decision to purchase, stay with us, and refer us to others. The scale lists three questions each buyer may ponder, which represent their "concerns."

3 Concern Questions of Cognitive Dissonance:

1. I wonder if have been fooled?

2. I wonder if they have spun me a lie?
3. I wonder whether there was something wrong with the deal I got?

Typically, our clients will not directly ask us these questions, but it does not mean that they are not thinking of them. While there may be a different answer to each, there is one underlying theme that is present if these questions enter our buyer's minds: a breakdown in trust.

Because most people have experienced buyer's remorse, they tend to have their guard up when someone is trying to sell them something else. Are you starting to see why "sharing" is a more relevant approach to selling? It is critical to attain the data that will allow us to make recommendations that do not cause buyer's remorse.

That data also allows us to avoid a similar phenomenon that occurs before the sale. Buyers may experience concerns during the sales process if they feel that they are being guided in the wrong direction. They get "cold feet" and some will stop taking your calls or returning e-mails. When the warm relationship goes cold, it is typically due to an erosion of trust.

Sales Spark:
When buyers experience cold feet, sales people need to warm things up by asking better questions.

MAKING YOUR RECOMMENDATION

The medical field is well aware of the impact that poor recommendations are having on their patients, their practices, and their industry. To start tackling these issues, especially regarding surgery mistakes, one of the main solutions requires mandatory "time-outs" in the operating room.

This allows medical teams to review patient records and surgical plans. In other words, it forces them to review their tactical information!

Tactical Info is the data required to fully comprehend the needs of our buyers and deliver relevant recommendations. It is the detailed information necessary to provide us the knowledge to guide our clients. The more in depth the data, the more relevant the recommendations. This information allows us to take three actions with our buyers.

Tactical Data Actions:

1. Share Insights
2. Provide Proposals
3. Support Strategy

Share Insights: As trust is established, you may learn about the exact product or service the buyer currently uses. This level of knowledge typically allows us to share some insights on improving what they already have. We are not selling, but rather, looking for the opportunity to share basic advice. Your insights will build more trust and allow buyers to begin sharing what they are interested in - what you offer.

Provide Proposals: Once we have shared some insights and gathered additional information to guard against cold feet and buyer's remorse, we can confidently make our recommendations. Proposals are an integral part of our sales system, allowing us to transfer our data into tactical action. Sales proposals are the main move in the knowledge game and a significant element in creating sales combustion. They are our prescriptions and we cannot afford to misdiagnose our buyers.

Support Strategy: For 3-D Sales Leaders, it does not end with proposals. As trust builds to higher levels, our consultative approach helps us to gather deeper information to provide more than a proposal for their present needs. As our relationship transforms and the buyer begins to view us as an expert resource for their needs, we are able to support their long-term goals and vision. When you support their strategy, you will often unearth tremendous new opportunities for you and your buyer.

Sales Spark:
Strive to gather the data to support your clients' future and you will no longer be stuck in the present.

DATA THAT IS NOT IN YOUR FAVOR

Time is a commodity that we cannot get back once it is gone. It is in our best interest to identify the information that will save us time. I see too many sales people chasing sales that may never happen. Their time should be invested elsewhere. Sometimes, there are buyer requirements that we may not be able to fill. No matter how much we focus on building relationships and developing trust, we will not land every sale.

That takes a lot of pressure off of us and saves us a lot of time, which we can dedicate to those who are looking to buy from us. It is imperative that our questions open up deeper levels of dialogue and provide us with the answers to understand the criteria to complete the sale. If we fail to gather all of the data required, we could merely be spinning the wheels of our sales vehicle... and going nowhere

Buyers are not required to volunteer their information, so we must be diligent in acquiring it. As a keynote speaker, I connect with many event planners. Hiring professional speakers for their events, they seek out people who deliver powerful, relevant messages. They want someone who can motivate and inspire, someone who can train and educate. I do all of that, so they must want me, right?

If their criteria might eliminate me right out of the gate, I must be careful of the time I dedicate to that sale. While I have spoken at many "Women's" events, some event planners may specifically be searching for a female speaker. That one piece of data is critical. If another event planner is looking for a speaker on leadership, I should qualify for that one, right? I speak on a wide-array of leadership topics, everything from delegation and communication to culture and accountability.

But if the topic is "Leading IT Teams During the Implementation of a New ERP System," I would not fully qualify for that role, nor do I attempt to be everything for everyone. Just because I cannot recommend a solution in the present, does not mean that I cannot support their strategy for the future. I know when to "Abort Mission" on current proposals and shift gears to their long-term needs. Never waste your time or theirs.

Sales Spark:
Never mistake courtesy for consent. Find out the real, decision-making information.

RANKING YOUR CLIENTS

As you begin to gather the discovery info, action info, and tactical info, you will start to have a better understanding of your clients. I rank my relationship with each client. How well do I know them? Where is our trust level? I need to know the data to better understand them and position myself to make better recommendations than my rivals.

The Trust Scale allows me to identify each buyer. Using a scale of 1-5, with 5 being best, I reserve my 5's for relationships with the highest levels of trust. I rank my wife and my mom in the 5 category. If I made a recommendation to my mom, our relationship should have enough trust developed that she should say "Yes" every time. If my mom goes to someone else - my competition - I not only have a sales issue, I have a significant trust issue.

Use the Trust Scale to provide a quick analysis of how strong your relationship is with your potential buyers. Are you able to check off the 5 box with any of your clients and prospects, or is your mom all alone up there? As you rank each buyer, give an honest assessment. Look for the data, the proof, to validate your ranking.

While we strive to develop 5's with each buyer, maintain lofty standards for that rank. You will likely have a lot of satisfied clients who rank in the 4's or even the 3's. Look at each rank as an opportunity to build the relationship to the next level. Instead of getting out with a client to sell more, try connecting to develop more trust.

Trust Scale:

Client: _____

    ☐ 5 Unwavering

    ☐ 4 Strong

    ☐ 3 Above-Par

    ☐ 2 Basic

    ☐1 Weak

WRAP UP YOUR DATA

What do we do with all of the data we have gathered? Most sales people do very little. Others will plug it into the CRMs and use it to identify their opportunities and how to "close" more sales. Most sales professionals completely miss the mark with accountability and limit their true potential, regardless of how much success they have already experienced.

Just look at the use of a CRM (Customer Relationship Management) and you will see that many are off target. Very few sales people use this tool to build relationships even though that word is in the title. The "relationship" aspect is typically missing. I rarely find sales professionals who track their relationships in their "relationship" software. Most use it to track the status of the sales.

All of your information must be wrapped up in accountability. I know, I am using the "A" word and to most sales people, accountability is like kryptonite is to Superman. That one little green rock can cause the world's greatest superhero to lose his powers and send him crumbling to the ground. But what if it no longer hurt him? What if it made him stronger? He would be unstoppable.

Would you like to be unstoppable? Most sales professionals answer "Yes" to that question, but it is estimated that only 60% of sales people are hitting their quotas (their goals). Accountability, when used properly, will allow you to harness the power of your data and make the necessary course corrections to remain relevant to your buyers and consistently exceed your sales goals.

Most salespeople have a misconception about accountability. Instead of using it as a tool to get better, they view it as micromanagement, a lack of trust between them and their leaders, or a way of people checking in on them to make sure they are working. Accountability, when used properly, serves one key focus in sales. It leads to action.

There is so much info that we *could* track, but what *should* we track? Most sales people suffer from too much or too little. While we can track everything from calls and appointments to proposals and revenue, we must look for the data that will move us to greater levels of action.

We must strive for voluntary accountability: reporting our efforts without being asked to. If you are an independent contractor, there is even more of an onus on you doing it, too. Accountability accelerates performance and increases engagement for every sales person. There are two types of accountability that will either stall your sales engine or drive your sales results.

2 Types of Sales Accountability:

1. Weak - leads to excuses
2. Strong - leads to responsibility

STATUS REPORTS

As sales leaders, we need to be accountable, not just to ourselves, but to the teams that support our efforts. Accountability is our performance data. It is our way of letting our team know what actions we are taking and how they are able to support our efforts. After eliminating the notion of weak accountability, we need to focus on strong accountability.

Three Keys to Strong Accountability:

1. Serves a Purpose
2. Forms a Partnership
3. Transforms Results

We know that there is an infinite amount of data to track. I have found that an aviation perspective serves best for understanding what to track. As an air traffic controller in the Marines, we were aware of the location of each flight. An aircraft was in one of four places. Our buyers are no different. Most aircraft are in the hangars - not flying (not buying). This represents people that are merely on our prospect lists.

Other aircraft are in flight and appear on our radar, just like a buyer that has shown initial interest. We track the blip, guiding them closer to our airfield. As aircraft lower their landing gear, they enter the ATA (Air Traffic Area), a 5-mile radius around the control tower. These flights (buyers) are in view and should be landing (buying).

Once the aircraft touches down and they are on the ground, there is still work to do. We need to taxi them in and take care of them. This is the equivalent of a buyer's commitment to your proposal. You have landed the sale. Congratulations, your communication and data has brought the flight in safely.

Sales Flight Status

Hangar	0-69%	The buyer has not moved forward
Radar	70-89%	The buyer has expressed interest
ATA	90-99%	The sale is within sight
Groud	100%	The sale has landed

Take the *Data Assessment* to determine how well you and your team are using the information needed for combustion. Rank each category on a scale of 1-10, 10 being best. Are you acquiring the highest levels of Discovery, Action, and Tactical Info? Do you know your clients better, understand your rivals, and deliver stronger recommendations? Have you wrapped it all up into powerful forms of accountability?

DATA Assessment

Are You on Target?		**Rank (1-10)**
D	Discovery	
A	Action	_____
T	Tactical	_____
A	Accountability	_____
		_____

Now, it's time to get your sales engine revving and have all of your pistons firing so you can accelerate your sales vehicle. It's time to create Unstoppable Gears.

PART III
UNSTOPPABLE GEARS

Life is like a ten-speed bicycle. Most of us have gears we never use.

~ Charles M. Schulz

PART III

Unstoppable GEARS

Increasing Your Horsepower.

If you want to get more than a gallop out of your sales performance, you should consider checking the horsepower of your engine. The concept of comparing machines to horses was refined into a scientific formula by Scottish engineer James Watt in the late 18th century. With the advent of the steam engine, he used the term to compare the output of horses with that of the engines that would replace them.

Watt determined that a horse had the power to turn a mill wheel 144 times in an hour. With a 12-foot wheel radius, the horse circled 2.4 times in one minute. Watt then added that the horse could pull with a force of 180 pounds. So, the formula looked like this:

$$P = W/T = F\,d\,t = 180\,lbf \times 2.4 \times 2\,\pi \times 12\,ft\,1\,min = 32,572\,ft \cdot l$$

Initially used to compare the power of a horse to steam engines, it later included the output of other types of engines. While there are other factors that contribute to the performance of an engine, it's power can be measured as 1 horsepower equals 550 foot-pounds per second. Horsepower allows you to define an engine's capacity for work. A 10-horsepower machine did the work of 10 horses - 10 horses you no longer need to feed, water, and take care of.

Still used in most car commercials today, horsepower is one of the first indicators of your vehicle's expected performance. What do you expect from the performance of your sales vehicle? How much horsepower does your sales engine produce? I have found that too many sales engines are performing as if they only have "ponypower," unable to do the heavy lifting required for true combustion.

GAUGING PERFORMANCE

Just as it is possible to increase your vehicle's horsepower through adjustments to air intake and upgrades to exhaust and electrical systems, you can also upgrade the horsepower of your sales vehicle. But to do that, we must determine how our engine reacts to temperature.

As we increase the performance of our sales engines, how will our sales teams react? It is critical to gauge their performance, and ours, as we shift into higher levels of performance. I have found that there are two distinct types of selling that sales people engage in: thermometer selling and thermostat selling. How do your sales people perform?

THERMOMETER Selling:	**THERMOSTAT Selling:**
REACTIVE	PROACTIVE
Succumbs to circumstances	Embraces the opportunities
Controlled by surroundings	Sets their own tone
Let's others pull them down	Lifts others up
Situational attitude	Pre-determined attitude

Both styles define the capacity of the person. Thermometer Sales Professionals focus more on their limitations, often hitting the brakes and hindering their true potential. But the Thermostat Sales Leaders focus on their untapped potential, spinning the gears needed to move them to action. Thermostat Sales Leaders operate at the highest levels of efficiency and are able to raise their performance "temperature" to achieve their desired outcomes, sometimes just by one critical degree.

1 DEGREE IS SIGNIFICANT

When we pour water into a kettle and place it over a heat source, great things are possible. Boiling water allows us to cook certain foods and it also kills bacteria, making some unconsumable water safe to drink. It also creates an energy source.

At 211 degrees, you merely have a pot of hot water. But at 212 degrees, a transformation occurs. That one extra degree causes the rapid vaporization of the liquid. The water enters a new phase as it becomes steam. One single degree creates an energy source. When the energy is put into an engine, it becomes a power source, which allows for the achievement of greater results.

Energy ➡ Power ➡ Results

Since horsepower was first used to describe the relations of power to steam engines, let's think about the impact that water could have on one specific vehicle - a train. More specifically, what could water do to a steam locomotive? If you are unable to achieve that one extra degree, you will be left only with hot water and your options will be limited. I suppose you could wash your sales train.

What happens if your competitor can achieve the one extra degree? He can move his sales train. It is imperative to become a Thermostat Sales Leader and create the energy needed for your sales engine. Convert it into the power needed to spin your sales gears and move your sales vehicle so you will experience new results.

Sales Spark:
Adjust your sales thermostat and experience the exhilaration of the power from the one extra degree.

ARE YOU LEAVING MONEY ON THE TABLE?

How important is timing for sales professionals? Critical! When a buyer is ready, you must be prepared. You cannot afford for your sales engine to stop functioning. But I have found that most sales people end up leaving so much on the table because they do not have a grasp on the timing of sales.

Keys to Sales Timing:

1. 50% of buyers choose the first responder.
2. 95% of buyers choose those who provide relevant touches.
3. 85% of buyers view 5 or more pieces of content.
4. 70% of buyers buy to solve a problem.
5. Most buyers are looking for a personal relationship.

Buyers will not wait for a sales professional to move on these five factors. If your sales engine does not position you to take action, you may watch more opportunities drive off with your rivals. Becoming a Thermostat Sales Leader allows us to do more than spin the gears of our sales engine - it allows us to make them unstoppable.

Too many sales professionals and sales teams try to achieve consistent results without consistently following a system. Those who operate without following a sales system are like Olympic athletes who try to get in shape without a regimented routine. Even great athletes cannot expect to see results just by showing up at the gym. Their performance is enhanced by their routines.

Your performance will be enhanced by your sales system. Although there are hundreds of selling strategies, I have found that there are five basic gears that allow sales engines to operate predictably and profitably.

The 5 Gears of Your Sales Engine, when operating in unison, will enable you to consistently develop new clients, earn more referrals, and maintain existing business, regardless of what industry you are in. They allow you to move in the right direction and be at the forefront of your buyer's thoughts when the time is right for action.

The 5 Gears of Your Sales Engine:

- Gear 1: Prospecting
- Gear 2: Contacting
- Gear 3: Presenting
- Gear 4: Set–Up
- Gear 5: Follow–Up

There are three keys that will not only supply your gears the combustion to turn but will make them unstoppable.

The Three Keys to Maintaining Unstoppable GEARS:

1. Achieving Ignition (Prospecting & Contacting)
2. Creating Momentum (Presenting & Set-Up)
3. Developing Velocity (Follow-Up)

CHAPTER 7

ACHIEVING IGNITION

Turn the key.

There is nothing more frustrating than turning the key and your car fails to start. But that's how many sales people begin each day. Now, imagine if your vehicle failed to perform 80% of the time. What would you do? First, you would probably be heading to a car lot to find a sales person who is not trying to "sell" and "close" you. Then, I'm sure you would trade it in.

While most people are not familiar with Italian economist Vilfredo Pareto, many are familiar with The Pareto Principle, named after him by management consultant Joseph M. Juran. In 1896, Pareto referred to the 80/20 connection, showing that approximately 80% of the land in Italy was owned by 20% of the people.

The Pareto Principle, also known as the 80/20 rule, the law of the vital few, or the principle of factor sparsity, states that roughly 80% of our results come from 20% of our efforts. It has been adopted to many facets, not just land ownership.

Distribution of Wealth: Global income reflects that the richest 20% of the world's population control about 80% of the world's wealth.

Taxation: In the U.S., roughly 80% of Federal income tax has been paid by the top 20% of earners, which parallels the above statistic.

Software: Microsoft noted that 80% of errors and crashes were resolved by fixing the top 20% of the most-reported bugs. It was also discovered that 80% of errors were found in 20% of the code. They also noted that 80% of code writing goes to the hardest 20% of the code.

Sports: 80% of the impact from training comes from roughly 20% of the exercises and habits of the trainee.

Occupational Health and Safety: 80% of injuries come from 20% of the hazards.

Sales: 80% of our sales volume comes from 20% of our client base.

While the principle may not apply to everything, we can see that there is enough evidence to suggest that 20% of our efforts yield 80% of our results. Conversely, 80% of our efforts only garner 20% of our results. So, the way I see it, is that we have a tremendous amount of untapped potential (80%) in our efforts, which can be refined and enhanced - ignited.

For transformational sales results, we need to achieve ignition. To successfully spark our sales engine, we are going to focus on two specific gears: Prospecting and Contacting. So, let's take a closer look at the definition of *ignition* to increase combustion every time we turn the key.

ig•ni•tion
noun

- The process or means of igniting a fuel mixture (such as an electric spark).
- The art or process of initiating combustion.
- The heating of a compound or mixture to the point of complete combustion.

REVVING IT UP

Showing up to your sales office ignites nothing. It's like sitting in your car after the engine fails to kick over. Too many salespeople take a reactive approach when contacting buyers to search for new business. While patience is a virtue, waiting for the next phone call to come in is not a solid strategy. Perhaps the reason that more inbound calls do not happen is because your prospects and clients are on the phone with your competitors!

Selling is a lot like fishing. The idea of a fish voluntarily jumping into your boat is exciting, but successful anglers consistently cast their lines to ensure a healthy catch. There are other people fishing for your buyers and far too many sales people fail to achieve ignition because they do not have a process for contacting people in a consistent and effective way.

When I ran the sales team at the media company, I knew that we needed to gather unparalleled data: discovery info, action info, and tactical info. Our buyers did not miraculously send us this data by chance. We needed to make the choice to start our day by turning the key.

Sales Spark:
Contacting is the key to success. But for it to operate properly we also need to spin our prospecting gear.

An initial contact can be sent with an e-mail or a LinkedIn message. But, like most sales professionals, our sales team agreed that the most important touch was a phone call. The live connection was the beginning of the sales cycle and it moved buyers out of the hangar and onto our radar.

Although we unanimously agreed about the power of phone calls, we did not initially experience the tidal wave of dialing I had hoped for. I needed us all to do more than just sit in our vehicle and hope for the best. We needed to turn the key and have contacting occur consistently.

THE 400-POUND PHONE

Teenagers are accustomed to hearing parents say, "Get off of your phone." According to an article by the Washington Post, "Teens spend nearly nine hours every day consuming media," and they do it, typically, on their phones. According a Kaiser Foundation study,

"Children between the ages of eight and eighteen spend an average of 7 hours 38 minutes a day with digital media. When the use of more than one digital device at a time is taken into account, they spend more than 10 1/2 hours a day."

These numbers seem too high to believe, but children are predominantly connected to their phones during most of their waking hours. This probably explains why I found 314,000,000 results on Google when I typed in "Keeping kids off of their phones." Understandably, most parents are struggling to keep their children off of their phones.

Conversely, most sales leaders are struggling to keep their teams on them. You know your people are not making enough calls. Period! At the media company, I needed my sales team to embrace their phones just as much as a teenager does. So, I began to look closely at our Contacting Gear and found two critical factors that prevented it from spinning regularly.

1. Our Prospecting Gear was stagnant.
2. Contacting time was not blocked out.

Prospecting and contacting work together. They go together like peas and carrots, Batman and Robin, peanut butter and jelly. Selling and succeeding. In sales, the phone is the outreach tool that gets everything in motion. But most sales people act as if the phone weighs 400 pounds. They struggle to pick it up and often find other things to keep them busy.

Sales Spark:
The phone is a sales tool to transform busy work into productive actions.

Keeping your Prospecting and Contacting Gears turning will increase your ability to expand your client base exponentially. To create ignition, let's analyze both gears so they become well-oiled - unstoppable.

PROSPECTING
The Art of Deciding Whom to Contact

When I think of prospecting, the image of an old man with a shovel and pick-axe comes to mind. With his tools in hand, he diligently searches for valuable minerals. Using his gold pan, he sifts for flakes of gold. Perhaps - just maybe - some nuggets. His success is based on his prospecting skills. He does not randomly begin digging. He decides where to stake his claim.

With the exception of Antarctica, gold is found on every continent on Earth. So how much gold is out there? According to the Thomson Reuters annual gold survey, their latest figure places the amount of gold at approximately 188,825 tons. All of the world's gold would fit into a cube with equal sides of about 68 feet. That is a lot of gold to search for.

Deciding where to look beforehand could be one of the best decisions the old prospector makes. How many potential clients are out there for you? Too many to get to all at once. That is why prospecting is the art of deciding whom to contact. Remember, one of the 3 D's is Decisions.

Sales Spark:
Prospecting is the number one decision you make every day and it dictates where you invest the rest of your time.

STAKE YOUR CLAIM

Salespeople often dive right into their contacting efforts but fail to achieve their desired results. Many work hard at turning their Contacting Gear, but put little thought into their Prospecting Gear. If your prospecting is motionless, you will have less success when attempting to turn your Contacting Gear.

Prospecting is much more than mindlessly dumping a phone book onto a piece of paper. Your Prospecting Gear enables the ongoing, detailed identification and analysis of people to contact: the 'who,' the 'why,' the 'when,' and the 'how.' Anyone can make a list of names, but very few can transform those names into satisfied clients.

Many salespeople can develop lists with dozens if not hundreds of names. But the idea of contacting that many people intimidates them, and understandably so. Below are three important questions that define a sales person's level of prospecting and the outcome of their prospecting list.

Three Key Prospecting Questions:

1. Level 1   Whom can I call?   (1-Dimensional)
2. Level 2   Whom can I sell?   (2-Dimensional)
3. Level 3   Whom can I impact? (3-Dimensional)

WHOM CAN I CALL? 1-Dimensional salespeople call buyers but fail to set an appointment. They call, merely to get through their daily phone calls, using more of a "checkbox" approach, but fail to achieve their purpose.

WHOM CAN I SELL? 2-Dimensional sales professionals call their prospects and only ask for the sale. Many buyers will start to avoid calls from people who offer nothing more than the opportunity to be sold and closed.

WHOM CAN I IMPACT? 3–Dimensional Sales Leaders identify people they can make an impact with. They are prepared to help their prospects to accomplish their goals. By focusing on an outcome like this, you are more likely to make an appointment and earn their business.

I prefer to create a prospecting list of people I can impact, not just call or sell. Your prospecting list is a work in progress – it is never complete. If your list stops growing, your business stops growing!

PROSPECTING LIST

It all starts with defining the ideal customer then finding and reaching out to them. The aim being to add people to your list who have both a need and the budget required for the product or service you offer. For a contact to make it to your prospecting list, filter them.

Three Prospecting Filters:

1. Targeting
2. Qualifying
3. Preparing

Targeting: In its simplest form, identify the clients you want to work with. What specific individuals, businesses, industries, or sectors do you need to connect with? Be clear!

Qualifying: What criteria do you have for your clients? Are you looking for a certain annual revenue size, team size, or market share? Be specific!

Preparing: A little research helps to determine what they already own and if it's in the same category as your product or service. Be prepared!

Operating in the cold market does not motivate most salespeople. Hence, they avoid calling. But if you have absolutely no connections, you may need to start cold, then warm them up with your dynamic contacting efforts (Gear 2). I prefer to start my prospecting list with my warm market and devote my energies to getting the word out to them. Understanding that there are far more people whom I do not know than people I do know, I encourage my personal contacts to introduce me to their warm market.

The best way to expand your list is by adding new names - people you do not have a relationship with. But how can you add the names of people you do not yet know? You enlist the support of the people you do know. They will melt down the barrier between your warm market and the cold market.

Even if you use a CRM, take the time to jot down the names of the people you need to connect with each day. You can use The 3–D Prospecting List (next page). It holds 25 names, so you may need three or four sheets to list your growing warm market. Perhaps you will need more than that!

BRAIN POWER

Having a written prospect list is a huge factor in your success, but here is a game-changing step for turning you prospect list into a combustion tool: Do it sooner. Too many salespeople "decide" who to call right when they pick up the phone and they miss the opportunity to use their brain power.

Most adults spend nearly one-third of their lives sleeping. Scientific American's article, *What Happens in the Brain During Sleep?* states, "When we fall asleep, the brain does not merely go offline, a dreamer's brain becomes highly active." What is your brain working on when you are dreaming? A recent study published in the journal, Current Biology, found that the brain processes complex stimuli during sleep, and uses this information to make decisions while awake.

Our brains process data and prepares for action during sleep, effectively making decisions while unconscious. By creating your prospecting list in advance and reviewing it at the end of the day, your brain will work to assist you in making better calls. Yes, you can contact someone without prospecting, but why would you?

Sales Spark:
To spin your Prospecting Gear at new levels, prospect the night before you call.

Prospecting enhances **Contacting**.

3-D PROSPECTING LIST

NAME	RATING	OUTCOME	DATE

CONTACTING
The Mastery of Setting the Appointment

I love it when I make a call to a prospect and before they say, "Hello," they enthusiastically yell out, "I want to buy something right now and I want to buy it from you!" Don't you love it when that happens? That is the miracle fish that jumps into your boat. I have done the math to prove that it does not happen enough to make a living.

Even the best laid-out prospecting list will not make the calls for you. Our ability to effectively and efficiently communicate is essential for ensuring that our Contacting Gear is spinning constantly. A lot is riding on our calls, but most fear doing it the wrong way or getting a "No," which can be major hurdles to overcome. The statistics on sales calls are not encouraging.

Below are the key stats on contacting:

1. Average sales rep can leave 25 hours of voicemails per month.
2. 80% of phone calls go straight to voicemail.
3. 90% of first-time voicemails are ignored.
4. Only 2% of cold calls result in an appointment.

No wonder most salespeople are hesitant to make a call. Even though my prospecting list was strong, I was reluctant to pick up my phone, too. When we are only trying to sell, that phone sure weighs a lot. But identifying our true purpose for the phone call helps us to overcome that fear.

Your Contacting Gear is meant to do much more than just allow you to speak to someone. It is designed to provide you with the opportunity to make contact with your prospects and set up a face-to-face appointment.

FEEDING TIME

While most salespeople hesitate to pick up the phone, some take the opposite approach and rifle through their calls, but still fall short on their outcome. Contacting is like feeding birds at the park. I once saw a young child, his hands filled with popcorn, run toward a flock of pigeons. There were dozens of them on the grass and all of them were hungry.

The idea of feeding them put a big smile across the boy's face. As he neared the birds, he screamed with excitement and threw his popcorn in the air. He certainly made 'contact' with the pigeons. He let them know he was there and had something great to offer them. Despite their hunger, they flew off without eating any of his popcorn.

The boy's grandfather watched his face turn from joy to sadness as a few feathers fell back to the ground. He knelt down and helped his grandson pick up the popcorn, then walked him over to a bench. As they sat, he told him to toss a few pieces out. The boy did so, and eventually the birds flew back for the popcorn. They continued this process until all of the pigeons had returned, including a few new ones.

Like most salespeople, the boy's intentions were good, but his techniques scared away his prospects. Has this ever happened to you? Have you ever been so excited about what you had to offer that you quickly picked up the phone, punched in a number, and showered your prospect with your 'popcorn'? We have all been there and experienced people going "silent."

The true purpose of contacting is to get you in position to transform your prospect into a client and to encourage your clients to trust you with referrals. Always contact to set the next appointment, or sometimes, the first.

Sales Spark:
The phone is a tool, best used to set up face-to-face appointments.

GETTING TO THE POINT

So, what is the best method of contacting? Any form of contacting that leads to an appointment is a useful form of reaching out. If you are able to send smoke signals and achieve great results, then keep sending those smoke signals. In order to set face-to-face appointments, I have used every form of contacting, but three ways work best for me. I have sent e-mails, made calls, or sometimes done a drop-by.

Regardless of my preferred method of contacting, my outcome is always the same: to set an appointment. While each method can help you to do that, it may take a combination of all three to accomplish it. Regardless of what industry people sell in, I have found a common mistake made by most sales professionals – they say too much during the initial contact.

Many keep a prospect on the phone for five, ten, fifteen, and even thirty minutes as they excitedly pitch their products. Some buyers are too polite to share their true thoughts: "I want off of this phone call." I have also seen e-mails that were pages of "valuable" information, but it took forever to get to the "are you available for an appointment?" question.

By eliminating your lengthy 'state of the union' speeches, you will have more valuable time to set additional appointments. Remember, you are striving to build relationships and the best relationships are built in person, face-to-face. I can tell my wife that I love her over the phone, but it has much more meaning when I say it in person.

 Sales Spark:
In sales, we are in the business of setting appointments. Become a professional appointment-setter.

Are there times when a prospect will want to stay on the phone and chat? Yes, but it is your responsibility to keep your Contacting Gear turning, set an appointment, then contact your next prospect.

Because most of my calls are made to get face-to-face time with my clients, I strive to limit the amount of time I am on the phone to two minutes or less. Consider the three key areas of contacting before you pick up the phone or send your next e-mail.

Three Key Areas of Contacting:
1. It's not a presentation
2. You are being graded
3. Respect their time

Contacting is not the best time to make a presentation – that falls under Gear 3. Call and say enough to pique their interest and leave the rest for the appointment. You are always being judged by your prospects. If you talk too long on the phone, how long are you going to talk in person? Have the utmost respect for their time when you call them.

If you are only able to visit with a prospect over the phone, or video conference, then that is a presentation. Make contact to set up the "appointment" call and be prepared to deliver a dynamic presentation. Try not to combine contacting and presenting into one phone call.

In addition to personally making contact with thousands of prospects, I have observed the contacting efforts of countless sales professionals. While most salespeople make calls with the best of intentions, filled with certainty and passion, they rarely achieve the results they were hoping for.

To increase performance, both your Prospecting and Contacting Gears must work together. If you are not fine-tuning both, you will rarely hear the sweet purring of your sales engine.

Contacting enables **Presenting!**

CHAPTER 8

CREATING MOMENTUM

Push the pedal.

Congratulations! You did it. You turned your Prospecting Gear and identified a buyer you want to work with. You reviewed your prospecting list the night before and put your brain power to work. Then, you spun your Contacting Gear and set an appointment. You turned the key, achieved ignition, and your sales engine is purring. So, now what? Now, it is time to create the momentum to move your sales vehicle forward.

To do that, let's take a look at the physics of the Momentum Principle, which governs nearly all motion. In very simple terms, this principle relates the "cause of motion," the interactions, or force to measure an interaction. The change in momentum is equal to the net force times the duration of interaction. It is also known as Newton's second law. Ok, maybe it is not so simple. But we all want to create sales motion.

In short, momentum is the product of the mass and velocity of an object. If "m" is an object's mass and "v" is the velocity, then the factor to calculate momentum is: $p = mv$. In order to move our sales vehicles, I prefer to use the Sales Momentum Formula. If "p" is Presenting and "s' is Set-Up, then the factor to calculate sales momentum is : $m = ps$. In short, sales momentum is the product of your presenting skills and set-up abilities.

> ### The Sales Momentum Formula
> *Momentum = Presenting x Set-Up*

Even with our sales engines running, our vehicles will not drive themselves. It's time to shift gears and put them in "drive." For transformational sales results, we need momentum. To successfully drive your sales vehicle, you are going to focus on two specific gears: Presenting and Set-Up. So, let's take a closer look at the definition of *momentum* to increase combustion every time we push the pedal.

mo•men•tum
noun
- Force or speed of movement, impetus, as of a physical object or course of events.
- Strength or force gained by motion or by a series of events.
- The force that drives something forward to keep it moving.

Combustion is all about the momentum you create. It's the simultaneous advancement of the sales process while building deeper relationships. By combining the strength of your Presenting and Set-Up Gears, you will communicate clarity as you share your message and commitment as you deliver the highest levels of excellence with your products and services.

Momentum is the result of a presentation that encourages your buyer to take action, and it continues to build as you move forward and set up the components to accomplish their goals. To move your sales vehicle, strive for deliberate acceleration. Deliberate acceleration focuses on the consistent, intentional actions required to make progress - to make an impact.

Sales Spark:
Avoid setting your sales vehicle on cruise control. Instead, focus on the deliberate acceleration needed for success.

PRESENTING
Moving From Content to Connection

Sales presentations come in all shapes and sizes. I have given thousands and I have observed many more. An unlimited number of tools exist to help make a great presentation. I have seen PowerPoint slide shows, dry erase boards, flip charts, easels, pictures, videos, and graphs. Some presenters wear suits, while others wear shorts and sandals.

Some people jump up and down on stage, while others stand as still as a robot. Some were loud; others were barely audible. Some lasted ten minutes while others took more than an hour. I have listened to men and women, young and old. I have listened to presentations in coffee shops, homes, businesses, and stadiums.

Presentations can involve a combination of the above styles. Some use more, while others use less. I have seen presentations succeed and I have seen them fail. Early in my career, I delivered presentations that did not result in momentum, even though I thought I did an outstanding job. Presentations that fail to deliver usually end the selling process at that point.

So what style is the most effective? The best presentation is the one that generates momentum. Every buyer is different. Not every style will work with everyone, so you must find the common ground between you and your prospect. You must be able to build rapport quickly, deliver a meaningful message, and leave your audience wanting what you offer. Because your presentation time most likely will be limited, that may seem like a lot to accomplish in one appointment. Welcome to sales!

Salespeople are easily intimidated to make presentations. After all, public speaking is considered by many as their number one fear. Some people fear dying less than speaking in public. While there is a lot riding on your presentation, the best ones should be as natural as taking a casual stroll along a beautiful beach. Everyone likes that image, even your buyers.

The key to creating momentum is not what you bring to the presentation, it is what your buyer leaves with. Your presentation is not a song and dance. It is your opportunity to communicate your belief level in what you offer and demonstrate your personal commitment to your client.

There is a good chance that everyone you want to sell to has already heard a presentation about related products from someone else. There is also a good chance that they will hear another presentation about similar products after yours. Turning your Presenting Gear is not about presenting your product better. Instead, it teaches you how to make an impact, which is what your prospect is largely basing their decision on.

Sales Spark:
When you are presenting, don't look for applause, look for approval.

YOUR MISSION

It was February of 1987 and I would be graduating high school in June. Like most seniors, I experienced a lot of excitement and anxiety about my future. My friend, Judy, had already enlisted in the Army and mentioned that she would begin basic training in the summer. Knowing that I wanted to serve our nation, too, she invited me to meet her recruiter.

Do you remember the first time you experienced a sales presentation? I do, although I did not feel like anyone was selling me. I remember that day like it was yesterday because my salesman did more than sell me, he made an impact in my life.

Judy and I stepped into the recruiting station in Pomona, California, which housed recruiters from each branch of service. As we walked into the Army office, I was greeted by her recruiter, a sergeant who seemed excited to meet me. He shook my hand firmly and shared about all of the opportunities that the Army provided. He handed me a tri-fold about the G.I. Bill, the VA Loan, and other benefits. There were a lot of tanks on his literature.

He needed to meet with Judy for a few minutes, so I wandered across the hall to the Navy office. A sailor greeted me and asked a little bit about myself, then started to tell me about the opportunities in the Navy. I received the same literature, except his had a lot of pictures of ships. The same thing happened with the Air Force recruiter. As you might imagine, his literature featured a lot of planes.

So far, things were going well. I met three enthusiastic, proud, and knowledgeable recruiters who all represented their branch of service at the highest levels. I also came away with the opportunity to earn many benefits. With my hands filled with literature, I walked to the end of the hallway. There was one office left.

I stepped up to the last office and looked in. No one came out to greet me. Instead, there was a Marine, seated at his desk. His office was meticulously decorated with Marine Corps items and posters. Sayings like "Semper Fi'" and "The few, the proud, the Marines" were all about. His pen glided across a piece of paper on his desk, then he looked up at me. I think I may have smiled. But he lowered his head and continued to write.

Ok, this was a bit different than the last three offices. A few seconds passed, although it seemed longer. He set his pen down and looked up. "Can I help you?" he asked. I tried not to show my nervousness and replied. "Yes." Not my most confident answer, I followed up with, "I want to learn about joining the Marines." He signaled with his finger and said, "Come in here."

I stepped into his office and right up to his desk. He stood up and looked at the literature from all of his competitors. What he said did not sell me. It did not close me. What he delivered was a single statement that made an impact. He believed it when he said, "We've got all of that stuff too. But becoming a Marine is not about what you get, it's about who you become."

"Do you feel that you have what it takes to be one of the best?" he asked. "I do" was my reply and then he shared all about his Marine Corps. That was my first sales presentation. It is the basis for how I shared my financial products, my media services, and now my professional development programs.

Sales Spark:
Do more than offer your "stuff." Share the impact that it will have in their business and in their lives.

Was my recruiter responsible for hitting his numbers? Yes, each recruiter must make mission. Was he accountable for his performance and results? Yes, he would ultimately answer to his commanding officer if his sales numbers were flat. Was he in sales? Yes, absolutely 100% yes! Recruiting is the sales arm of each branch of service. But my recruiter made an impact that has lasted for over thirty years. How long does your impact last?

HOW TO PRESENT LIKE A RECRUITER

To properly turn your Presenting Gear, you must know your client well enough to be able to develop a case–specific presentation that works for them. While presenting, you will be constantly asking questions and gathering data to best support their needs and create more momentum.

Too often, salespeople regurgitate the same presentation material regardless of what type of presentation they are giving. There is nothing more distracting than a one–dimensional presenter. Although there are several ways to deliver your message, I have found that there are really just three types of presentations.

The 3 Types of Presentations:

Primary Presentations:

This is an introduction about you, your organization, and what you offer. This presentation allows you to use your Fact-Finder and start gathering better data (Discovery Info).

Proposal Presentations:

After assessing their needs, you will present your recommendations to identify how your offerings will improve their business/life. Using your Fact-Finder, you will gather deeper data (Action Info).

Purpose Presentations:

After you begin to set up your clients' initial products and services, you will share ideas about how you can support their future needs, too. Using your Fact-Finder again, you will gather visionary data (Tactical Info).

While my focus and questions may differ for each type of presentation, my desired objective is the same: to make an impact. Too many sales people get off track when presenting. They begin with good intentions but end up with little to no momentum created. I do not merely show up and hope for the best. I use six specific steps to guide me and keep me on course during each presentation.

Six Steps to Successful Presenting:

1. Stay on Time
2. Build Rapport
3. Ask Questions
4. Identify Challenges
5. Share Solutions
6. Identify Next Steps

By following the six steps, you will deliver a professional presentation that will influence and motivate people to take action. Each primary presentation should lead to a proposal presentation, which should lead to a purpose presentation. This happens over time, not overnight. You need momentum and trust to continue to build.

The quality of your presentations often determines whether a prospect buys from you or from one of your competitors. While taking each of the six steps to stay on course, you can also enhance each presentation by focusing on the Six Secrets of Presenting.

Six Secrets of Presenting:

1. Practice your delivery
2. Dive deeper with your questions

3. Speak their language
4. Avoid overload
5. Control content
6. Use support materials

SCRIPTS

When I was in the film industry, "script" was not a bad word, but it is in sales. Most sales people reject the idea of using scripts and I appreciate their concerns. They typically have three negative perceptions about scripts. They feel that they are unnatural, they come across as fake, and they are awkward to use.

There is a lot to be said about their use. When used properly, scripts increase your performance during your presentation. A well-crafted script, when used properly, enhances your delivery. They identify your best practices - the optimal way to describe what you sell. They also allow you and your team members to maintain the highest levels of consistency with your messages. As an actor, you have the opportunity to win an Oscar for your performance; for your delivery of the words and meaning in your script.

Every great movie starts with a script, even though you may be required to ad lib. Every great presentation does, too. You just cannot merely read it. You must deliver it with the highest levels of passion and belief. A powerful script will allow you to rehearse and improve. It will allow you to ask better questions and exude confidence.

Sales Spark:
The person asking questions guides the conversation and the most confident person wins the conversation.

AFTER THE PRESENTATION

We are typically not paid to make presentations. We are paid when they turn into a sale, something we can set up for our buyer. Even the best presentations don't always yield a sale right out of the gates. You may hear "No." When I do, I hear a shorter way of the buyer saying, "<u>Not</u> Yet." When your presentation does not turn into something to set up, you must start spinning your Follow-Up Gear (Gear 5) to relevantly reconnect and position yourself for your next appointment.

Have I made sales without presenting? Yes, every so often a sale jumps into my fishing boat. But I circle back, to deliver a dynamic presentation, to make sure my client stays with me. Your presentation is always about much more than how your products and services will work for them, it is about how you will work for them. What level of service do you provide when you set up what you recommended?

Presenting provides **Set–Up**

SET-UP
When the Real Sales Work Begins

Do you know what's more important than making the sale? Keeping it! You promised your prospect the world during your presentation and now it is time to deliver. You have undoubtedly put a lot of work into getting the sale. There is absolutely no need to lose it. In sales, the real work starts after the sale is made!

According to Newton's third law, for every action there is an equal and opposite reaction. This happens all too often in most sales scenarios: a reaction occurs that is opposite of what is expected from the buyer. Their sales professional quickly moves on to the next best thing. They barely turn their Set-Up Gear.

In the fast–paced, highly competitive selling environment, very few salespeople allocate enough time to this gear. Their Set–Up Gear remains still because they do not understand its significance. Set-up is your ability to exceed your clients' expectations during the completion of the sale and the momentum created for new opportunities. There are three keys to always keep in mind.

Three Keys of Set-Up:

1. Differentiate yourself from your competition
2. Don't move onto the next sale too quickly
3. Deliver excellence

Every new client compares us to their former sales person. We are most often judged by the quality of our delivery, not just by the content of the presentation. We cannot afford to be perceived as someone who moves on to the next sale too quickly. Many clients feel abandoned right after the sale. Our Set-Up Gear provides us with the opportunity to deliver excellence.

Sales Spark:
Your Set-Up Gear allows you to cultivate your relationship with your client by providing you the opportunity to shine.

Completing a sale is much like planting the seed of a fruit tree. While each seed carries with it the possibility of a bountiful harvest, you must pay particular attention to cultivating it during this crucial phase. There is nothing more disappointing than preparing the soil and the seed, only to experience a lack of growth.

HIGH STANDARDS

The Set–Up Gear is designed to increase your chances of keeping the business that you worked so hard for. Many salespeople consider the sale complete once their client gives a verbal agreement, while others use a written commitment as a sign that the sale is final. Some use time periods to consider it complete, often when it has been on the books for a few months. It is not uncommon for others to view the arrival of their commission checks as the signal that the sale is complete. What are your criteria?

There is only one sign that I use to gauge the completion of my sales. Referrals! I do not consider a sale completed until I have received at least one referral from my new client and that referral has become a new client. Those who refer business to you rarely remove business from you. Keep your standards high regarding the signs you observe with your sales.

Completing the sale is not a 'set it and forget it' technique. By focusing on your Set–Up Gear, you will pay attention to all of the steps, processes and systems necessary to properly set up your new clients. Your post–sale involvement throughout this process is crucial, so maintain the highest standards with three critical sales components.

Three Keys of Set-Up:
1. First Order
2. Account Status
3. Next Order

Just as the first year of a child's life is fragile and needs constant supervision, so too does your relationship with your buyer once they transform into your client. They are observing every step you take and grading you on how you set up their first order, how you maintain their account, and how you handle their next order.

Do not overlook this phase, which can easily disconnect the connection you made with them during previous appointments. Too many sales people haul up a great catch and mindlessly toss the fish onto the dock, expecting their operations team to process it flawlessly. My Set-Up Gear was not just to build the relationship with my client, it was critical to build my relationships with the people supporting my sales efforts.

I have sold in three different industries: financial services, broadcast media, and professional development. I have also trained sales leaders in virtually every other industry. Although the set–up requirements for each product and service vary, they have one thing in common. They occur after the sale is made.

STILL DECIDING

A sale never ends with a handshake, it only begins to turn your Set-Up Gear. During this phase, you are being closely watched and you cannot afford to lose the momentum of this gear. Your presentation has turned into a commitment from your buyer. Will you deliver them your commitment?

Your set-up results will answer this question and allow them to continue to make the decision to remain your client. Properly turning your Set-Up Gear provides three distinct opportunities for increasing your results.

Three Opportunities of Proper Set-Up:
1. Guide your client
2. Process their order
3. Gather referrals

Guide Your Client: The care and attention you must show a new client is the same that you would for a newborn child. When you let a child take their first steps without your guidance, there is room for unnecessary bumps and bruises. In the beginning phases of client relationships, you will want to take every step with them.

Process Their Order: As you guide your client, you must simultaneously ensure that their order, which you recommended, is processed and delivered at the highest levels of excellence. A mistake in the set-up phase of a new client can be catastrophic to future business.

Gather Referrals: I am always aware of what I am doing, what I am saying, and how I am taking care of my clients. Because the greatest compliment in the world of sales is a referral. How you get a referral says a lot about your relationship with your client and how well you have been turning your Set–Up Gear.

Sales Spark:
If you have not started to gather a lot of referrals, put more effort into properly turning your Set–Up Gear.

Set-Up fosters **Follow–Up**

Chapter 9

Developing Velocity

Shift your thinking.

It always happens when you are least expecting it. You're enjoying the drive, cruising to your favorite song, and taking in the beautiful view. Then, your steering wheel starts to pull to the right and you hear that undeniable flapping noise that can only mean one thing. Applying some extra force to your steering wheel, and guiding your car onto the shoulder, you step around to the other side to verify what you already know. It's a flat tire.

Like most people, you have been there before. Although it is frustrating, you make the long walk to your trunk and mentally prepare to swap out your spare tire. But it is gone. In fact, if you own a brand-new car, you might discover that there is a high likelihood that it was never there in the first place. According to a recent study conducted by the American Automobile Association, 28 percent of 2017 model-year vehicles aren't equipped with spare tires. What? Why?

Some spare tires started to disappear when automobile manufacturers began trying to save weight, yes weight, and bolster government-mandated fuel efficiency. In 2016, AAA stated that more than 450,000 stranded motorists called them because they did not have a spare.

Since spare tires go unused about 85 percent of the time, they seemed like an easy solution to weight savings and were pulled from some models without anyone noticing. Well, until they had a flat tire. Without that one special tire, your drive does more than stop, it could leave you stranded and way off schedule.

Many sales professionals treat follow-up like a spare tire. For some, their sales vehicles are not even equipped with one. Others merely stuff them in their trunks and they remain unused until they have an emergency. Unlike that neglected piece of rubber, your Follow-Up Gear will do more than help you to experience ignition and momentum. It is the catalyst for breaking barriers.

To successfully develop velocity, you must do more than take your Follow-Up Gear out the trunk of your sales vehicle. You must consistently spin it. So, let's take a closer look at the definition of *velocity* to turbo-charge your engine as you shift gears and surpass your rivals.

vel•oc•ity
noun

- Rapidity or speed of motion; swiftness.
- Speed imparted to something.
- The rate of motion of a body expressed as the rate of change of its position in a particular direction with time.

Properly turning your Follow–Up Gear involves various forms of contacting, but this gear has a much different purpose than your Contacting Gear. While the outcome of contacting is to set the next appointment, the outcome of follow–up is to exhibit your true commitment to your buyers.

I have discovered that follow-up is the most underutilized gear in the sales system. But if you are dedicated to turning your Follow-Up Gear, then I am going to caution you to fasten your seatbelt, because you are going to move beyond your limitations and your expectations as you increase the velocity of your sales vehicle.

FOLLOW-UP
The True Testament of Your Commitment

There is a first time for everything and today is that day. You get to say the F-word in a sales book: F***. But you finally get to use the word in accordance with its true meaning. Yes, I am talking about

"Follow-Up." Although many sales professionals may view it as a four-letter word, this gear holds a tremendous amount of power.

So why is it not used as much? Salespeople fail to turn their Follow–Up Gear because they do not have a proper understanding of what follow–up is. Follow–up is another word for keeping your commitment. Consistently turning your Follow–Up Gear allows you to communicate your dedication to serve your existing clients and potential clients.

My sales seminars are always packed with hungry salespeople, who want new strategies to elevate their results. Inevitably, we discuss follow-up. I ask, "How many of you feel that follow-up is critical to your success?" Of course, nearly every hand shoots into the air. Naturally, I want to identify the best techniques in the room. But I pre-frame my next question.

"Imagine that I'm your potential buyer and you delivered a great presentation, but I have not returned your last call. What is your best follow-up?" And then I add, "But it cannot be, 'I wanted to follow-up, I'm circling back, I wanted to touch base, or I'm just checking in." There is typically some guilty laughter and then the room goes silent. Acknowledging the importance of follow-up and actually providing it are two different things.

Sales Spark:
Follow-Up is more than a way to let a buyer know you are there, it is the best way to let them know you care.

STOP BEING A PEST

After admitting that follow-up is critical, I ask why so few sales people follow-up. Their answers are not only similar, but they identify a gap in their systems. When I hear things like, "I don't want to be a pest" or "I don't want to bother them," I know that their sales vehicles are running on fumes. When your follow-up techniques are pestering or bothering people, you are using the wrong tools to turn your Follow-Up Gear.

There is too much riding on follow-up to leave this gear in the trunk. While we will be uncovering the strategies, techniques, and tools required for relevant and meaningful follow-up touches, let's first take a look at three absolutes: the three realities about this critical gear.

Three Realities of Follow-Up:
1. The most common complaint   (from the buyer)
2. The most common excuse   (from the seller)
3. The fortune is in the follow-up   (for the buyer and seller)

The Most Common Complaint: The first reality is the perception from the buyer. When asked about why they did not choose to go with a salesperson, one of the most common answers given is the lack of follow-up. The follow–up abilities of the salesperson was a determining factor in their decision–making process. Not even the most powerful presentation or the most dynamic communication skills will help you when you fail to turn your Follow–Up Gear.

Some buyers were annoyed that the salesperson did not call them back, while others were disappointed they did not receive information they had been promised. What shocked me was the frequent mention that some salespeople failed to deliver a proposal, illustration, or price bid that the buyer had requested. There was a lack of follow–up and it cost the sales person dearly! Failure to follow–up with a potential client is like a fisherman who fails to reel in his catch. Why cast your line in the first place?

Sales Spark:
When a buyer encounters a lack of follow-up, they also experience a lack of commitment.

The Most Common Excuse: The second reality is the perception from the seller. Following up with a buyer seems simple enough. With credibility at stake, why do some salespeople drop the ball? All you need to do is to make the call, send the e–mail, or deliver the information, right? There are always plenty of excuses for neglecting a follow-up step, but these are merely the symptoms of the deeper follow–up issue – the lack of commitment.

The two most common excuses for not following up on a client request are usually, "I forgot…" or "I was too busy…" When you forget about your buyer, it won't take long for them to forget about you. Your clients expect you to keep their business front and center of your activities. It should be important for you to serve them, not forget them. Salespeople who forget to follow–up on client requests will rarely have many clients to forget about.

Also, no one is too busy to improve their sales results. This excuse sends the signal that your client is not your highest priority. Salespeople who are too busy to follow–up typically do not have that problem for long! When you stop your Follow–Up Gear, you allow sales to slip right through your fingers and into your competitor's hands.

Salespeople do not start their day trying to discover new ways to sabotage their businesses, but they certainly do just that when they fail to follow–up with a client request. How many of your potential clients are waiting to spend money with you right now? Unless you effectively turn your Follow–Up Gear, you will never know.

YOUR FORTUNE AWAITS

The Fortune is in the Follow-Up: The third and most critical reality is not a perception. It is a proven, solid fact. Because most salespeople do not have relevant follow-up touches, their gear fails to spin, and they fail to attain the abundance of opportunities in front of them. Their fortunes go to their competition. Your lack of follow-up is their gain.

To measure the success of your Follow-Up Gear, gauge your performance and your results. *Statistics* is the science of developing and studying data and there is an abundance regarding follow-up. We use various methods for collecting, analyzing, interpreting and presenting information.

When it comes to the exact science of analyzing a sales professional's performance and results, I am going to say that it would be difficult to get the exact science of follow-up, but some of the popular statistics are listed below regarding performance and results.

Follow-Up Performance:

1. 48% of Sales Professionals Do Not Follow Up
2. 25% of Sales Professionals Make a Second Contact and Stop
3. 12% of Sales Professionals Make Three Contacts and Stop
4. 10% of Sales Professionals Make More Than Three Contacts

Follow-Up Results:

1. 2% of Sales are Made on the First Contact
2. 3% of Sales are Made on the Second Contact
3. 5% of Sales are Made on the Third Contact
4. 10% of Sales are Made on the Fourth Contact
5. 80% of Sales are Made on the Fifth to Twelfth Contact

Do these statistics represent every salesperson? No! But I must say that after twenty years in sales, they certainly come close to the many I have met. The key is for you to increase your follow-up performance and results. Improve the velocity of your sales vehicle by adjusting the speed of your Follow-Up Gear. Are you faster than your competition?

Some studies show that the average salesperson takes up to three days to connect with a buyer after their inquiry. That is a lot of time for your competitors to outpace you. The Harvard Business Review published an article discussing the follow-up of leads, from 2,241 U.S. companies, and the results are shocking, but not uncommon.

- 37% responded within an hour
- 16% responded within 1-24 hours
- 24% took more than 24 hours
- 23% never responded at all

Your Follow–Up Gear is designed to turn in unison with your other sales gears. I have seen salespeople follow–up too much and I have seen others follow–up too little. Having the right balance will enhance your ability to turn all of your other gears more effectively. Your Follow–Up Gear must start turning as soon as each of your other sales gears begin to move.

Sales Spark:
Follow-up is the simplest, fastest way to grow your business, but it takes discipline to spin this gear.

WHEN TO FOLLOW-UP

I am confident that by now you see the need to turn your Follow–Up Gear if you want to achieve greater results. But many salespeople leave follow–up in the air, creating room for error and dissatisfaction.

So, when is the best time to follow-up? There are only two types of follow–up:

- Responding to buyer requests
- Initiating action

While both types are critical to achieving consistent results, we must place a sense of urgency on returning phone calls, sending information, or delivering important documents. When a buyer request is made, the timing for follow–up is immediate. In addition to responding to requests, we must also initiate action, then follow-up to keep our engines on.

Most salespeople stop pursuing a potential client as soon as they hear, "I'm happy with my current salesperson." They may be happy currently, but most clients want to remain happy. When your competitor drops the ball, and they will, you need to be there to pick it up and run with it. By turning your Follow–Up Gear, you will be able to be on the forefront of your buyer's mind when their Relationship Wave is low with your rival.

I am often asked, "How many follow–up calls does it take to complete a sale?" I always tell them the same answer, "Only the last one." It is up to you to discover which one that is. I have completed sales after the first call and I have completed sales after the tenth call. Too many salespeople give up after a certain number of tries. Some people quit after the third call failed to produce results, while others toss in the towel after the first call.

Although there are varying statistics on this, most people tend to finalize their buying decision somewhere between number five and twelve. Wow, that's a lot of follow-up. Yes, that's a lot, but there are sales waiting for you. Do you have the determination to make the follow-up call that will complete the sale? I am committed to making at least twelve touches.

When I met with Frank from South Park, he too was happy with his current vendor. But I remained persistent for more than two years until he finally called and said, "I need your help with tonight's episode." I jumped at the chance and we flawlessly completed the work. In addition to handling that order, I had earned the entire show and became their new sales rep. It took more than two years and twenty-two touches, but it paid off. It always does, if you turn your Follow-Up Gear.

Sales Spark:
If you're not prepared to make 12 touches, you should never make the first.

FOLLOW-UP TOOLBOX

You can earn business from someone who has a great relationship with your competition, if you are willing to perform the appropriate follow-up. To earn South Park's business, I never called Frank to "check in, touch base, or circle back." I opened my Follow-Up Toolbox and made relevant and timely touches. Understand that your prospect is most likely receiving follow-up calls from your competition. What distinguishes your follow-up from theirs? What's in your toolbox?

FOLLOW-UP TOOLBOX

• Company Overview	• Videos
• Articles	• Service Sheets
• Industry Events	• Lunch/Coffee Invitation
• Blogs	• Humor
• Testimonials	• After Hours Events
• Website Pages	• Community Outreach
• Conference Calls	• Referrals

Below are examples of what I keep in my Follow-Up Toolbox to help me build relationships and trust. These tools show my commitment level.

Each follow-up touch could be an e-mail attachment, an insert into the body of the message, or a link to a webpage. Regardless of what I was sending, I always started my follow-up touch with something like, "While you are considering Think GREAT for your sales training needs, I wanted to send you this:

"Article about team engagement..."

"Video that shares the importance of having a sales schedule..." "Blog about communication..."

"Link to what people are saying about working with us..." "Comic strip to start your week..."

"Story about your (favorite sports team, hometown, movie)..."

Just as each wave on the ocean is unique, so is each selling situation. Every buyer is different, and you cannot afford to send your follow-up touches to mindlessly check off the box. Each touch has the power to build relationships or erode trust, so they must be relevant, meaningful, and have the personal touch added where appropriate.

Sales Spark:
A great follow up touch does not always need to be about selling.

Follow-ups are too important to leave them to chance. I schedule my follow–ups as if they are appointments, putting each in my calendar and treating them with the same focus as a presentation. Follow–up does more than just keep your name at the forefront of a prospect's mind, it allows them to refer you to their warm market, sometimes before they have become your new client.

FOLLOW-UP LEADS TO REFERRALS

Not keeping a commitment or neglecting to honor a client's request happens frequently in every industry. I have experienced it firsthand as a client. I once had a pool contractor tell me that he would give me a quote to upgrade my pool filter – I received no call. I waited for weeks to receive information from my tax preparer – I received no information. I once requested a proposal to have my home painted – I received no proposal.

By failing to turn their Follow-Up Gears, they failed to keep me, or add me, as a client. Not only did they lose my business, they lost my respect for them and any notion that I would connect them to a friend or colleague. It costs little to spin your Follow-Up Gear, but the cost of not spinning it can be significant.

The idea of a fish jumping into your boat seems unlikely. What about having a school of fish jump in? We must be dreaming, right? When you develop relationships that send you referrals it's just like that. It is also a sign that your Follow-Up Gear is not only spinning but delivering the message that it is good to do business with you.

In sales, we need to take the actions that stack the deck in our favor, and earning referrals is the ultimate deck-stacking strategy. A warm referral will break down any "cold" barriers and infinitely increase your velocity. How beneficial is a referral? Whereas only one out of twenty prospects buy from you, the game changes with referrals.

The Velocity of a Referral:

- 1 out of 6 Referrals buy from you – 300% greater
- Referrals buy up to 3 times more
- Referrals stay 4 times longer
- Referrals are 2 ½ times more likely to refer you

TIMING YOUR FOLLOW-UP

Have you ever eaten seven apples in a single day? For most of us, the answer is "No," even though we are all familiar with the old adage, "An apple a day keeps the doctor away." I believe the saying suggests spreading out your healthy eating habits, not cramming them all into one day. One of the most common questions I am asked is, "How often should I follow-up?"

Just like eating fruit, properly spaced-out follow-up steps yield greater results. Just as each touch must be relevant, each touch must also be properly timed out to make the full impact. The frequency of your follow- up steps is critical, especially considering that up to twelve touches, sometimes more, may be required to convert a buyer into a client.

Because the magic of follow-up typically begins around the fifth touch, I divide my Follow-Up Campaigns into two phases:

Follow-Up Frequency Phases:

1. Phase 1:   Tactical Follow-Up   (Steps 01-05)
2. Phase 2:   Strategic Follow-Up   (Steps 06-12)

Steps 01-05 are the tactical, short-range touches designed to build trust as you state the date and time of your next step. The completion of each relevant touch sends a message of your true commitment level.

Steps 06-12 are the strategic, long-range touches that differentiate you from your competition. Each meaningful and valuable touch, from your Follow-Up Toolbox, keeps you at the forefront of the buyer's thoughts.

Sales Spark:
Each follow-up step is a link to the next touch, guiding your prospects along a pathway of mutual trust and respect.

GETTING YOUR FOLLOW-UP GEAR TO TURN

Every follow-up situation is unique, so you will need to design your campaign to support your developing relationships. Below is an example of how I implement Phase 1 to get my Follow-Up Gear turning.

Step 01 (Day 01) - E-mail:

An introductory message with an attached overview of our company/services. I mention that I want to learn more about their goals and I lead to the next touch by stating, "I'll call you in a couple days, unless you have a time that would work better."

Step 02 (Day 03) - Call:

Most calls go to voicemail, so I mention, "As promised, I wanted to give you a quick call to set up a time to get together." I acknowledge the attachment sent for review and I lead to the next touch: "I'll send an e-mail with a couple of dates and times to get together."

Step 03 (Day 05) - E-mail:

I acknowledge the message I left and add a few options of times to connect, possibly over a cup of coffee or at their office. I add an additional attachment, typically of a specific service we offer or a link to one of our videos. I lead to the next touch: "I will call next week."

Step 04 (Day 09) - Call:

As promised, I call to set up an appointment. Once the appointment is set, I lead to the next touch: an e-mail confirmation.

Step 05 (Day 10) - E-mail:

The e-mail confirmation goes out, along with another relevant attachment or a link to our website.

Within a two-week time period, the first five tactical touches have been completed and I have established a foundation of trust. Step six may likely be the first face-to-face appointment. I will gather data and begin to map out the strategic touches necessary to encourage the buyer to choose me.

A quick way of determining how well you are spinning your Follow-Up Gear is to assess how (and if) you receive referrals.

- You do not ask... you do not receive (A Missed Opportunity)
- You ask... you do not receive (Build the Relationship)
- You ask... you receive (On the right track)
- You do not ask... you receive (Developing Velocity)

Take the GEAR Assessment to determine how well your sales gears are spinning. Rank each gear on a scale of 1-10, 10 being best.

GEAR Assessment - Are you Moving?

	Are Your Gears Spinning?	Rank (1-10)
1	Prospecting	_____
2	Contacting	_____
3	Presenting	_____
4	Set-Up	_____
5	Follow-Up	_____

Are you achieving ignition, creating momentum, and developing velocity?

Where do you rank?

00-25   Sales Vehicle is Coasting
26-40   Sales Vehicle is Rolling
41-50   Sales Vehicle is SPEEDING

GEARS

It takes ten times the effort to develop a new client as it does to maintain an existing one. Turning all of your sales gears will do more than just create new business. Each will help you to keep business on the books. By focusing on your sales gears, you can systematize your selling efforts, regardless of how complex the sale is. Your sales engine allows you to achieve repeatable, predictable success.

You do not need more sales gears to experience greater results; you need to consistently increase the size of the five sales gears you are already turning

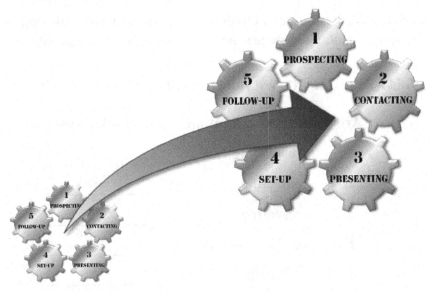

Follow-Up moves **Everything**

Now let's talk about how the best sales engine performance is associated with the structure holding it all together.

PART IV
UNMATCHED STRUCTURE

Growth is always essential... you want to make sure you're growing. Putting in place all of the right structure to be able to ensure growth.

~ Susan Wojcicki

PART IV

UNMATCHED STRUCTURE

A Power Source of Unlimited Potential.

To the ancient Greeks the Olympic Games were held in the highest regards. Staged in Olympia, these events were filled with blood and passion, screaming fans and extraordinary athletes. The Olympic Games were one of the highlights of the Greek culture and they endured for nearly twelve centuries before coming to an end. It took over 1,500 years for the modern Olympics to return. But in 1896, the first games were held, appropriately enough, in Athens, Greece.

Since then, the world's elite athletes converge every four years to compete. More than two hundred countries send thousands of athletes, who all share the same outcome. Weighing only 412 grams (0.9 pounds), there are about 400 gold medals available between the Summer and Winter Games. Athletes do not strive to win the silver or bronze. They spend a lifetime of training to bring home the gold.

So, what are the odds of becoming an elite athlete? Well, according to the NCAA, your odds of coming out of a university and being drafted by an NFL team are 0.03%. The NBA is slightly tougher at 0.02%. But what about an Olympic athlete? The U.S. sent 49 swimmers to the Rio Games in 2016, out of 362,320 swimmers registered with USA Swimming and spread out across nearly 3,000 teams. The odds of making that team? 0.0013%.

The Olympics is a game of extreme sacrifice and prestige, and there is no shame in winning a silver or bronze medal. However, there can be only one gold medalist. For those who do not win the gold, it goes to their rivals and they may wait another four years for their next shot. To win, athletes must prepare, mentally and physically, possessing an unbreakable mindset. But their actions leading up to the games do not happen randomly.

Each successful athlete is provided the structure necessary to support their efforts and enhance their skills. How important is structure? The U.S. Olympic Training Centers (OTCs) were created as facilities for these elite athletes, some living there for months or years during their training. They provide the structure for success.

SALES WEAKNESSES

When salespeople fail to hit their goals, the natural tendency of their supervisors (coaches) is to focus on the weaknesses of the sales professional. They address the "problems" with the person, but often fail to acknowledge the "problems" with the sales structure supporting the person.

There is much merit in assessing your sales "athletes" deficiencies and understanding what holds them back. Objective Management Group assessed more than 1 million salespeople over the past 26 years and discovered certain factors, "Sales DNA Weaknesses," that cause sales people to become uncomfortable and fail to perform.

Six Sales DNA Weaknesses:

Difficulty Recovering from Rejection   39%
Becomes Emotional   66%
Need for Approval   68%
Discomfort Talking About Money   72%
Non-Supportive Buying Cycle   72%
Self-Limiting Beliefs   86%

While there is plenty of truth to these weaknesses, I believe that they are the symptoms of a greater issue. With the right structure, most sales professionals are able to overcome their limitations. Having a strong sales structure will not only eliminate weaknesses, but transform them into strengths, allowing your sales athletes to fine-tune their skills.

Sales Spark:
The key to a successful sales operation is structure.

STRUCTURAL INTEGRITY

To unleash your team's abilities, creating the right structure is essential. Only providing a phone, a CRM, and some brochures will not suffice. You must build the support system to enhance, encourage, and empower your people. So, let's take a closer look at the definition of *structure* to expand the power of your sales engine and increase your odds for a gold medal.

struc•ture
noun

- The action of building.
- Something arranged in a definitive pattern.
- To give form or arrangement to.
- Something constructed.

According to TeamUSA.org, "The mission of the U.S. Olympic and Paralympic training sites is to provide athletes with access to additional resources, services and facilities, while providing an elite athlete training environment that positively impacts performance." They built the structure to support their outcome: winning.

Sales Spark:
Your structure supports your outcome.

Sales structure refers to the organization of team member duties and sales support functions. Knowing your outcome will allow you to create the infrastructure to keep it all together and achieve higher levels of sales combustion. Below are some common sales outcomes. What is yours?

- *New Business*   • *Volume per Client*   • *New Markets*
- *New Clients*   • *Increase Profits*   • *Retention*

When outcome is not clearly defined, existing sales configurations tend to provide little support. Weak sales structures not only impact the ability to capture opportunities, but they inevitably lead to significant financial consequences for the organization. We cannot afford to fall short on the structure required for championship performance and results.

Sales professionals who operate in a weak structure often have difficulty describing how the basic components of their sales environment work, such as:

- *Compensation*   • *Workflow*   • *Support Roles*
- *Territories*   • *Lead Assignment* • *Marketing*
- *CRM/Software* • *Resources*   • *Team/Leaders*

A weak structure undermines even the strongest salesperson. If Olympic athletes performed in a weak structure, what would their results be like? They would probably fail to win the gold and may struggle to win the silver or even the bronze. It may impact their ability to even qualify to compete. Most sales professionals have their eye on the gold medal but spend far too much time on the bench.

SALES OLYMPICS

At the media company, our sales team started with little experience in sales and they could have easily been hindered from the Six Sales DNA Weaknesses or anything else that got in their path. I developed a structure to enhance our skills, improve our mental fortitude, and boost the success of all of our sales activities.

Sales structure supported our outcome and kept the sales engine running at high levels. Initially focused on doubling sales, our structure allowed us to triple annual revenue, increase profits, expand into new markets, and much more. All of this would have been impossible with a weak structure.

Sales Spark:
A weak sales structure leads to confusion and wasted time.

If sales were an Olympic sport, how would you want your team to perform? Does your structure support them "bringing home the gold"? While Olympic athletes get one chance every four years for glory, sales professionals have the opportunity for a fresh start each day. With the right structure, you and your team will create dynamic "Olympic" sales combustion.

There is little difference between Olympic champions and Sales champions. To win the gold, your sales structure needs three building blocks: a plan, a schedule, and an environment for success. Will you provide the structure your team needs to become sales champions?

The Three Building Blocks for Unmatched STRUCTURE:

1. Your Plan
2. Your Schedule
3. Your Environment

CHAPTER 10

YOUR PLAN

Are you planning to win?

In 1972 a crack commando unit was sent to prison by a military court for a crime they didn't commit. These men promptly escaped from a maximum-security stockade to the Los Angeles underground. Today, still wanted by the government, they survive as soldiers of fortune. If you have a problem, if no one else can help, and if you can find them, maybe you can hire the A-Team.

On Jan 23, 1983, The A-Team burst onto TV with this introduction and I was hooked. Action - and a lot of it - was guaranteed every week. At school the next morning, I talked about each adventure with friends and it was not uncommon to hear someone emulate Mr. T by saying, "I pity the fool." No matter what challenges the team faced, at the end of every episode, there was one guarantee. That guarantee was that the A-Team would win.

In the world of selling, there is only one guarantee. That guarantee is that people will buy. Unfortunately, there is no guarantee that they will buy from you. The competition to win each sale is fierce and your competitors will usually not give up without a fight. Salespeople compete every day. Some win and some lose. Some drive their sales vehicles, some stall. Some plan and some don't.

Mr. T drove his infamous black and red van in every episode. Doing more than engaging in car chases and crashing through gates, his vehicle was part of their plan. Yes, the A-Team had a plan. Facing insurmountable odds, Colonel Hannibal Smith always gathered his team and mapped out a way to win. Sometimes, using just a stick, he drew out their plan in the dirt.

How important was their plan? It sent the A-Team into action and they claimed victory against all of their rivals. Their enemies never stood a chance because they did not have a plan of their own. At the end of every episode, it happened. Col. Smith, usually bruised and banged up, lit his cigar and proudly announced, "I love it when a plan comes together." I wish I heard more salespeople say the same thing. Unfortunately, most operate with no plan - not even lines in the dirt.

Sales Spark:
A sales plan is your roadmap to guide your sales vehicle and keep you on track with your goals.

A SIMPLE CUP OF TEA

I met with a salesperson who was struggling to reach his goals, but he could not figure out what he was doing wrong. He was energetic, passionate, and had no fear of talking to people. Trust me, he could talk! He seemed perfect for sales, but his results were lacking. I met with him in his office to discuss his performance.

His desk was cluttered, but there was also evidence to suggest that he had been working. Piles of Post–It Notes, papers, contacting sheets, a few bids, and a box of tea bags made it nearly impossible to see his desktop. After some small talk, I asked him about his forecasted numbers, but he was not certain that he could reach them.

I looked over a stack of reports: his year–to–date numbers, his opportunities, his projections, and his customer list, to name a few. But I focused more on the salesperson sitting across from me than on the numbers that currently represented him. He had a lot of potential, but he was not living up to it. He was making phone calls, sending out e-mails, and scheduling presentations.

But he was not able to pull it all together, which is not uncommon for many salespeople. So, I asked, "Can I see your plan?" When he answered, "What plan?" I knew where the problem was, so I asked if he would pass me the box of tea bags from the corner of his desk. He quickly reached for it and handed it to me. I pointed to the back panel of the box and read the instructions to him:

- Pour boiling water over tea bag
- Brew for 3–5 minutes
- Remove tea bag and stir
- Add a lemon slice, honey, or milk

I asked him why there were detailed instructions on his desk about making tea but none about making sales. He was silent, but he nodded his head slightly, which communicated volumes to me. There was evidence of great intentions on his desk, but not a single bullet point to help him achieve his sales goals. He needed a sales plan, a set of instructions to achieve sales combustion in his engine.

I would like to say that his situation was unique, but it is all too common. Many salespeople have less substance in their sales plans than in the instructions to make a simple beverage. Aren't your sales goals more valuable to you than a cup of tea?

SALES PLANS

Because sales is the lifeblood of any organization, having a plan for the sustainable growth of the department makes absolute sense. Just like a marketing plan, financial plan, or an operational plan, the sales plan is a critical component of the long-term strategic vision of any business. Based on my strategic planning book, *ELEVATE*, I use our Business Elevation System (BES) to help business leaders to design and launch their Flight Plans.

During the Flight Plan creation, I have the opportunity to learn a great deal about how business leaders, their teams, and their organizations operate. But I quickly discover that many lack a formal sales plan. Although they have lofty goals for their sales teams, they lack a written plan describing the performance required for success. But that is not the only plan lacking.

Most individual salespeople do not have their own plans to accelerate their personal performance. Sure, they have some goals or quotas listed, but not a plan on how to accomplish them. To keep your sales engine firing and your sales vehicle heading in the right direction, it is crucial to have a sales plan for each salesperson.

What does a sales plan do for you? You will win more sales, keep your clients, and develop an ever–growing list of new referrals. A plan transforms your sales vehicle into an aircraft, so you can achieve higher levels of success, reach new heights, and experience a view like you have only dreamed of. It will elevate your skills from sales driver to sales pilot.

The A-Team often parked their van and boarded an aircraft to fulfill missions in far-off, remote locations. But that required Captain Murdock to escape from a mental hospital to pilot the aircraft. Of course, he escaped every episode, with the help of the team. Afraid to fly, Mr. T's character, B.A. Baracus always proclaimed, "I ain't gettin' in no plane with that fool." But he always fell for the spiked milk trick and ended up asleep for the ride.

To succeed in sales, we need to do more than just draw lines in the dirt. We must also do more than just show up each day to work. We need a detailed action plan to enhance our performance. You cannot afford to wait for somebody to plan your success. You must make planning a priority.

Sales Spark:
Don't wait for someone else to create your sales plan. Take initiative and make it happen.

KISS

While "time" is a common excuse for not having a written plan, I believe it goes deeper. While every sales leader and salesperson usually agree that it makes sense to have a plan, most do not have one. Creating a plan seems daunting, regardless of how much value is attached to it. I like the acronym K.I.S.S. when thinking about planning: Keep It Simple, Salesperson.

At the media company, we were able to achieve and sustain growth through a powerful plan that was supported by every leader in our company. We experienced over 300% growth by launching new services, developing top-tier clients, and expanding into new markets and locations, to name a few. Our plans were successful, but I realized quickly that there were two sales plans needed to fly our sales vehicle.

The Two Sales Plans for Combustion:

1. Team Plan
2. Individual Plan

Team Plan: I am always amazed when a sales leader has no plan for their department and wonders why they did not hit their sales goals. Not having a team plan is like riding a bike while wearing a blindfold. You will probably achieve some momentum and ride for a while, but you are more likely to go the wrong way and inevitably crash.

The team sales plan allows you to identify the high-level strategic revenue targets, promotions, pricing, new markets, team structure, and the strategies and techniques to get there. It is a powerful tool that provides clarity and buy-in from your sales team and other company leaders. It has the ability to unify people under a common vision and mission. At the media company, our first team sales plan launched in 2004 and helped us to grow 23.99% in annual revenue that year.

The following year, as we fine-tuned our plan and team, we grew nearly 65% in annual revenue. Our team sales plan detailed our objectives, high-level tactics, target clients, and identified potential obstacles. It mapped out what we needed to accomplish our goals. But most importantly, our people had a deep understanding of how to support our plan.

Sales Spark:
A plan is a visual representation of your goals. For success, make your Team Sales Plan more visible to your team.

Individual Plan: I am always amazed when a sales professional has no plan for their performance and wonders why they did not hit their sales goals. Not having a plan for your personal performance is like sitting in a fishing boat without any fishing gear. You are merely along for the ride and it is highly unlikely that you will catch much. Unless, of course, that miracle fish jumps in your boat.

Most sales people perform like they are along for the ride. Having a personal plan will detail your important goals and the steps needed to get there. Each individual plan increases the likelihood of success for the team plan. They all work together.

A sales plan, both for the department and for the individual sales professional, should be short, simple and to the point. While it is important to clearly articulate long-term objectives, I have found that the most effective sales plans guide our focus onto the immediate actions required for consistent success. Too many salespeople work on things in the present that do not support their future.

Your plan should never hamper your progress. Yes, you need to invest time into putting it together and implementing it, but no one ever said it had to be done during productive business hours. I did most of my planning, for the media company, after hours.

Sales Spark:
You earn a living from 9-5, but you create lifestyle before and after!

YOUR SALES PLAN

Over the years, my sales plans have evolved. Beginning in the financial services industry, they provided clarity and helped me to stay focused, overcome my challenges, and develop new clients. In the media services industry, they provided strategy and allowed us to successfully fuel our long-term vision while supporting the success of our sales team.

My sales strategies have evolved into the Sales Impact System (SIS), to help sales leaders build dynamic structures for high-level combustion. One foundational component of the SIS is the individual sales plan, the Sales Impact Plan (SIP), which allows sales professionals to power their own sales engines. Below are the three components required to build a complete sales plan:

SALES IMPACT PLAN (SIP):

- *STRATEGIC VISION*
  - *Personal Vision Statement*
  - *3-5-year goals*

- *TACTICAL MISSION*
  - *Personal Mission Statement*
  - *1-year goals*

- *IMMEDIATE ACTION*
  - *Personal Action Statement*
  - *90-Day Goals*

Most sales people leave their goals to chance. Too often it's because they do not know how to create a plan, or they lack the resources. You no longer have that problem. Use the templates on the next three pages to complete your Sales Impact Plan.

STRATEGIC VISION: Start with your *Personal Vision Statement*; your declaration about where you want to go and who you will transform into.

My personal vision statement is, "To enrich the lives of military families in a world free of cancer." This is my vision - it guides all of my actions.

List your 5-year, then 3-year goals. Set more than just a desired income. Identify important goals about growth, new opportunities, lifestyle enhancements, charity work, or improvements in your community.

TACTICAL MISSION: Add your *Personal Mission Statement*; the essence of what you currently provide your clients and how you operate now.

My personal mission statement is, "To help our clients achieve greater results, no matter what circumstances they face." This is my mission - I strive to accomplish it each day.

List your 1-year goals. While the final goal you set should state your desired income for the year, the others should focus on tactical enhancements, such as targeted new clients, customer satisfaction improvements, and workflow solutions to increase efficiencies and effectiveness.

IMMEDIATE ACTION: It's time for your *Personal Action Statement*; what you are committed to do on a daily basis to reach new levels and accomplish your mission and achieve your vision.

My personal action statement is, "To constantly improve and go above and beyond the call of duty every day." I must take this action to stay on course.

List your 90-day goals and the purpose of each. This is where the rubber "leaves" the road and allows your sales aircraft to take off. These goals need to be all about performance, performance, and more performance. These are the immediate actions that will get your sales vehicle moving at new speeds, such as more calls, more qualified appointments, and more proposals.

SALES IMPACT PLAN

STRATEGIC VISION

Personal VISION Statement:

_____

5-Year Goals:

• _____ • _____

• _____ • _____

• _____ • _____

_____

3-Year Goals:

• _____ • _____

• _____ • _____

• _____ • _____

SALES IMPACT PLAN

TACTICAL MISSION

Personal MISSION Statement:

_____

1-Year Goals:

- _____   - _____

- _____   - _____

- _____   - _____

- _____   - _____

- _____   - _____

- _____   - _____

SALES IMPACT PLAN

IMMEDIATE ACTION

Personal ACTION Statement:

_____

90-Day Goals:

- *Goal 1:* _____
- *Purpose:* _____

- *Goal 2:* _____
- *Purpose:* _____

- *Goal 3:* _____
- *Purpose:* _____

90-DAY RACES

For your Sales Impact Plan to be effective, it must have definitive time parameters. I use the power of 90-Day Races as the foundation for my sales plans. To maximize the effectiveness of your plan, keep the vision of your long-term goals in mind and operate within 90-day blocks of time. Successful salespeople target a specified date range to operate in.

This is a concept I discuss in great detail in my book, *The GOAL Formula*. I have found that people have the ability to stay focused for about 90 days. In fact, they can enhance more than their business during that time period, they can elevate their lives. I discovered this benefit firsthand when I was eighteen years old. I stepped off of the bus at the Marine Corps Recruiting Depot in San Diego, California, as a raw recruit.

Boot camp was filled with numerous mental and physical challenges. But ninety days later, I marched across the parade deck and graduated with my platoon as a U.S. Marine. The steps between our goals and our results were *planned* out with precise detail. Our drill instructors left nothing to chance and harnessed the power of a ninety–day plan. They scheduled our time to transform a group of undisciplined civilians into hard–charging Marines. Your sales plan will lead to your sales schedule!

What could you do in 90 days? By operating within 90-day blocks of time, your plan will transform your sales efforts into sales combustion. I have used 90-Day Races to reach my objectives in the military, in the financial services industry, and in the entertainment industry. Now, as a sales coach, I use this concept to develop sales leaders, from nearly every industry, to achieve their desired results.

Sales Spark:
Connect multiple 90-Day Races so your sales vehicle continues to move toward your long-term vision.

By setting up your plan in 90-day increments, you can course-correct as needed, develop beneficial habits, eliminate bad habits, and stay on track with your actions as you pursue your results. As you develop your plan, I recommend that you share it with as many people as you can. The more people who know about your plan, the more likely you will stick with it. Do not treat your plan like a top-secret document, keeping it away from everyone. Instead, enlist the support of people you know, and they will help to sustain your efforts. No one does it alone.

In the financial services industry, I used 90-Day Races to stay focused on my plan. It allowed me to become a top producer, recruiter, and trainer. In the media industry, I utilized back-to-back 90-Day Races with my entire sales team to bring our sales plan to life. We not only accomplished our goals, but we tripled our annual sales.

The question is not, "Does a 90 Day Race work?" The question is, "Will you create the plan necessary to enhance your sales vehicle and use a 90-Day Race for your goals?" The next 90 days are coming. What are you going to do with them? If you want your sales performance to improve, then work your plan! Your plan will not only help you to stay on track with your goals, it will separate you from your competition and will help to accomplish transformational sales results.

If your sales business is not growing, it is dying. Your plan will make sure that your sales pulse remains strong and that your career does not flatline. In addition to having a solid plan, your structure needs to include a schedule. While many salespeople may claim that a routine will reduce excitement and spontaneity, world-class champions disagree.

Every salesperson wants to go from point 'A' (their important goals) to point 'B' (their desired results). Each action in between needs to be planned and scheduled to support them. Let's take a closer look at fortifying your structure with a powerful schedule so you can always bring home the gold.

CHAPTER 11

YOUR SCHEDULE

Maximize each day!

We were there for only ninety days, but the images of our drill instructors will stay with us for the rest of our lives. Barking in our faces, yelling all day long, and pushing us to the breaking point, every enlisted Marine endured the non-stop intensity of their DI's. From morning 'til night, and often more than that, they were with us. We spent 13 weeks with them, in a well-structured environment, designed with one purpose: to make us Marines.

Despite the awkward start to boot camp, we learned how to walk, talk, and act like Marines. We were trained to march, fire our weapons, rappel, and swim. We were taught Marine Corps culture, heritage and traditions. Divided into three phases, Marine Corps boot camp was an integral part of the plan, with all paths leading to graduation day.

To accomplish their mission, the Marine Corps must graduate about 600 Marines per week. Every week, they hit their goal. In charge of the plan were our hard-as-nails drill instructors. Failure was not an option to them and it was not a wise choice for us. But our DI's knew that not everyone would make it; not all recruits would earn the eagle, globe, and anchor.

Drill instructors understand the importance of structure. Just like the U.S. Olympic Training Centers (OTCs), boot camp is designed for success, although it does feature more yelling. DI's stay committed to the plan, focused on building the next generation of Marines to carry on the Corps' legacy. To do so, each day is maximized to its full potential. DI's not only run a tight ship, they follow a schedule for success.

Every day is vitally important during recruit training, so nothing is left to chance. There was zero down time. We woke up, made our bunks, ate at the chow hall (breakfast, lunch, and dinner), ran or marched everywhere, trained for drill maneuvers, cleaned our weapons, attended classroom instruction, hand-washed our uniforms, negotiated obstacle courses, swam, stood for inspection, showered and prepared for the next day.

Each day, we had at least sixteen hours of non-stop activities. How do drill instructors keep everything together? How do they ensure that each day is productive? The secret is under the wide brims of their campaign covers, also known as "Smokey's," also known in civilian terms as hats.

One day, while doing countless push-ups in the dirt, I looked up to see Sgt. Hughes remove his cover for a brief moment. He pulled out a 3x5 card, glanced at it, placed it back in, then secured his cover atop his tightly shaved head. He barked a few commands and our platoon formed up and we marched to our next objective.

The 3x5 card listed our daily schedule. Our time was mapped out so each moment was an investment in our growth. Every minute supported the outcome of the plan and our drill instructors were unwavering with that tool. What would your results be like if you followed a schedule like that?

No matter how good you think you are, you cannot sell something yesterday. Today is all we have to work with, so we need to schedule it effectively! Each day is about 1% of our 90-Day Races, so we must make them count. The success of our plans will depend on how well we are able to control our time. The best way to maximize each day is by scheduling it. When we control our time, we control our success.

Sales Spark:
A sales schedule is like a fishing net, but instead of catching fish, you capture time.

THE MISSING LINK

When the owner of the media company shared with me that he wanted to double sales, he quickly acknowledged that he did not have a plan to get there. He did have the beginning of a sales team, but it currently consisted of one person, their sales manager. Although he had good intentions, he also lacked a plan. Their entire sales operation was based out of his small office.

It appeared that he was in the field on appointments, because he was rarely there. But when a prospect called in for him, no one knew exactly where he was. In his office, there was some evidence of "selling." There were notepads, but with minimal notes. He had client applications for requesting credit, but they were all blank. There were some pre-filled out order forms and some client correspondence on his desk. Like most sales people, I believe he was trying.

One critical component was missing. No matter how much I searched, I could not find his sales schedule. I'm not talking about his calendar with some random appointments listed. I am talking about a daily schedule that guided his performance. Without a schedule we are reactive, in a world that demands proactive.

Like most sales people, he did not even have a simple 3x5 card, mapping out his day. When he was in the office, he seemed busy. But his "busy work" did not translate into the results needed to double sales. Not even close. He was busy, but not productive. He had things in his calendar, but a calendar is not a schedule. Not only did this sales team need a plan, they needed a schedule.

 Sales Spark:
A calendar allows you to schedule activities. A schedule provides you the structure to optimize your time.

IN VS. ON

Because part of my background was in sales, I presented the owner with a sales plan. We needed to build the structure to support his outcome: to double sales. The plan consisted of having more than one person selling, designing a sales office, creating a sales system, targeting new accounts, and most importantly, developing a schedule to maximize our time.

It was an incredible, life-changing experience to build an entire sales system from the ground up and watch it grow. The ultimate key to sales success is time. Like most salespeople, our sales manager was working in sales, but he was rarely on top of his results. Busy work would not get us to our goal, but productive actions would.

Sales Spark:
"Busy" salespeople often have plenty of time available to make excuses.

In sales, we are often bombarded with so many things that can take us away from selling: e-mails, phone calls, inquiries, issues, reports, and the list goes on. Although each action may support sales, we must learn to distinguish the three types of actions that occur in our day.

The 3 Sales Actions:

- OUT   Time Wasted   Negative Actions
- IN   Time Spent   Important Tasks
- ON   Time Invested   Priority Objectives

OUT: These actions send our sales aircraft spiraling downward and cause us to get off track. Examples of "OUT" actions: surfing the internet, connecting with unqualified prospects, preparing orders (if you have a team for that), too much research, and too much time talking in the office.

IN: These tasks are important and help to keep our sales vehicles moving forward and staying on course with our goals. Examples of

"IN" tasks: returning client calls and e-mails, submitting proposals, and effectively communicating with team members about orders and accounts.

ON: These objectives are a priority and elevate our sales vehicles to new levels of growth and success. Examples of "ON" objectives: working your Sales Plan, making new outbound calls, setting new appointments, asking for referrals, and providing high-level follow-up.

| OUT | IN | ON |

While it makes sense to eliminate OUT actions, too many salespeople continue to hold onto them. Without a schedule, they also tend to focus their attention to their IN tasks before they tackle their ON objectives. They get it backwards. In a sea of infinite possibilities, we must narrow our actions down to our priority objectives.

Sales Spark:
Priorities drive performance, so schedule them first.

On the next two pages, you will see the exact daily schedule I created for our sales team at the media company. It allowed us to schedule the actions that yielded the greatest results. These blocks of time were essential, each day. We may not have been as unwavering as a drill instructor, but we followed the schedule as closely as possible. Use the template to start scheduling your time. It's all about progress, not perfection.

SALES TEAM SCHEDULE
DAILY AGENDA

Your time must be well invested!

Have a can-do attitude.

Follow the Sales Schedule to stay on track with your goals.

8:30 am	Walk-Through – Check current orders
9:00 am	Morning Meeting – Review the Numbers
9:30 am	Prep Time

- ☐ Tours, Lunches, Special Events
- ☐ Bids & Special Projects
- ☐ Follow-up / Top clients
- ☐ Visits, Top Ten, Cookies & Flowers

10:00 am	Phone Zone

- ☐ Thank You for your business
- ☐ Top Ten: New Calls, Referrals
- ☐ Follow-up, Existing Client Base

12:00 pm	Power Lunches
2:00 pm	Walk-Through – Check current orders
2:30 pm	Field Visits
4:00 pm	Afternoon Meeting – Success Stories
5:00 pm	Wrap-up the Follow-up
5:30 pm	Super-Star Activities

Become a master of the schedule – put yourself in front of more clients.

SALES IMPACT PLAN

DAILY SCHEDULE

Your time must be well invested!
Have a can-do attitude.
Follow the Sales Schedule to stay on track with your goals.

_____   _____

_____   _____

_____   _____

☐ _____

☐ _____

☐ _____

☐ _____

☐ _____

☐ _____

☐ _____

_____   _____

_____   _____

_____   _____

PURPOSE

Rather than just setting the schedule and hoping for the best, I identified the purpose of each block of time. If you cannot define it, you will likely not achieve it. Once the schedule was understood, everyone was encouraged to "Max out each portion of the Sales Schedule."

WALK-THROUGH - 8:30 am: Each sales rep was expected to know the status of their client orders and a brief walk through of the facility allowed them to orchestrate necessary actions for success and provided crucial information for follow-up calls during Phone Zone.

MORNING MEETING - 9:00 am: After the walk-throughs, we conducted a short Sales Meeting to review the previous day's actions, project the current day's results and set a level of high energy. Each meeting started by sharing our personal vision statements.

PREP-TIME - 9:30 am: This was an interactive time for our Sales Team. Their Fact-Finders provided them with plenty of areas for research and strategizing. We prepared all necessary aspects of our tours, lunches, dinners, drop-bys, presentations, events, etc.

PHONE ZONE - 10:00 am: Game Time! We had two hours to make as many well-executed contacts (not just dials) as possible. Utilizing a pre-planned Top Ten List (prospecting the night before) to max-out our calls, we connected with existing clients and prospects. Our goal was to set as many new appointments as possible.

POWER LUNCHES - 12:00 pm: We need to eat, so we turned it into an opportunity to meet with new and existing clients. Yes, power lunches are that powerful! Try not to eat alone! If they did not have a power lunch, I encouraged them to grab a quick bite and get back in the field!

WALK-THROUGH - 2:00 pm: Repeat a walk-through to analyze new work.

FIELD VISITS - 2:30 pm: More Game Time! We had two and a half hours to make as many well-executed visits and drop-bys as possible. A powerful Phone Zone helped guarantee more face-to-face visits.

AFTERNOON MEETING - 4:00 pm: If you were not still in the field, we gathered to share our "success stories" with the rest of the Sales Team!

WRAP UP THE FOLLOW-UP - 5:00 pm: We put the final touches on our daily activities to ensure that all elements of current orders, projects, and proposals were transitioned to the appropriate team members. This was the time that we prepared our Top Ten List for tomorrow's Phone Zone!

SUPER-STAR ACTIVITIES - 5:30 pm: Super-Star Game Time! So many great relationships are built after-hours, at special industry events or dinners. This is when the magic begins and your client relationships developed to incredible new levels. Only Super-Stars work after hours! If you want to get paid like a Super-Star, you have to perform like a Super-Star!

SCHEDULING THE GOLD

How important is a schedule? To Olympic swimmer, Michael Phelps, it was a priority. Each day consisted of eating, swimming, resting, weight-training, and meditation. Phelps and his coach, Dave Bowman, left nothing to chance. They identified the optimum time blocks for each action and scheduled them. The result: 28 Olympic medals: 2 bronze, 3 silver, and 23 gold (the most gold medals in the history of the Olympics). What does your daily schedule look like?

To schedule the gold at the media company, I not only set the stage for daily actions, but I identified the weekly expectations. One of the most valuable forms we used was our Weekly Performance Report. The next two pages show the exact report we used, followed by a template for you and your team to use to create your own weekly expectations and identify the actions your company needs to win the gold.

WEEKLY PERFORMANCE REPORT

WEEKLY	GOAL	M	T	W	T	F	TOTAL
New Calls:	50	——	——	——	——	——	——
Follow-Up Calls:	50	——	——	——	——	——	——
Drop-Bys:	25	——	——	——	——	——	——
Tours:	5	——	——	——	——	——	——
Demos:	5	——	——	——	——	——	——
Lunches:	5	——	——	——	——	——	——
Super-Star Activities:	5	——	——	——	——	——	——
Bids:	2	——	——	——	——	——	——
Proposals:	2	——	——	——	——	——	——
New Clients:	2	——	——	——	——	——	——
1st Orders:	5	——	——	——	——	——	——

**Where performance is measured...
performance increases!**

SALES IMPACT PLAN

WEEKLY PERFORMANCE REPORT

WEEKLY	GOAL	M	T	W	T	F	TOTAL

**Where performance is measured...
performance increases!**

In our sales manual, I described the benefit of the Weekly Performance Report by stating: "The greatest way to accomplish something is to first commit it to paper. By projecting out your week in advance, you and your supervisor will be able strategize ways to help you hit your projections."

It allowed our sales team to project their activities for the upcoming week. By looking at each week in advance, our team was able to use their sales schedule to maximize their time. The structure of the form was simple:

WEEKLY	- identify the actions that lead to success
GOAL	- set the expectation on weekly performance
MTWTF	- track the results from each day
TOTAL	- did you hit your goal?

The Weekly Performance Report enhanced our effective use of the Daily Schedule. There is no doubt that it takes discipline and accountability to use these tools. But we were able to do more than just schedule our days, we supported the outcome: to double sales. Our results: we tripled sales. Imagine the possibilities as you eliminate "busy" work and your entire team begins to schedule "productive" work.

EXPONENTIAL GROWTH

Perhaps the most used Latin phrase is *Carpe Diem*. Well, it is the most spoken, but not the most used. Translated today to mean "seize the day," it was taken from book 1 of Odes (23 BC), by the Roman poet Horace. More accurately translated, he was suggesting to "pluck the day," for it is ripe.

If you fail to schedule each day, how can you seize them? How can you pluck the ripe fruit before your competition pulls it from the tree and devours it? Each day is a powerhouse of unlimited potential and possibilities. But most sales people waste them away.

It is often the repetition of the small things that lead to the greatest rewards. While many sales people find other things to keep them busy, some set a specified number of calls to make each day. They follow their schedule and let their actions compound, creating exponential growth. Let's take a close look at what we really have to work with in a single day.

1 Day is Equal to:

- 24 Hours
- 1,440 Minutes
- 86,400 Seconds

Is it possible for you and your team members to each complete ten daily, well-placed calls to qualified potential clients? If your answer is "Yes," you have the potential for exponential growth. Contacting 10 people per day is the beginning of the magic. Just 10 calls per day equal:

10 Daily Calls ➔ 50 Weekly Calls ➔ 2,600 Yearly Calls

When training, Michael Phelps swam about 50 miles per week - about 2,600 miles per year. But it all started with "plucking" each day. Identify your weekly volume, then break it down daily and become unwavering about your schedule. Be the sales champion you are destined to be.

Without a schedule, any numbers are just wishful thinking. With a schedule, you will bring home the gold. There is one more component to finalize the structure necessary for success. To create the highest levels of buy-in from your sales team and everyone supporting your sales goals, it is time to unify your culture and create an environment of dynamic sales combustion throughout your entire organization.

CHAPTER 12

YOUR ENVIRONMENT

Have Your Cake and Eat it, too.

According to Henry Ford, "Enthusiasm is the yeast that makes your hopes shine to the stars. Enthusiasm is the sparkle in your eyes, the swing in your gait. The grip of your hand, the irresistible surge of will and energy to execute your ideas. You can do anything if you have enthusiasm." How important is enthusiasm in sales? Try selling without it and you will quickly find out. But how can you regularly spark it?

Recruiting, the sales arm of the Marine Corps, is challenging and known to be the toughest, non-combat job they have. I have had the opportunity to share my goal-setting and sales strategies with recruiters across the nation, and I have to agree. To make mission, recruiters, like any successful sales professional, adhere to their system, invest long hours in prospecting and contacting, and sharing the story of their beloved Corps.

They follow-up with thousands of high school students and work their way through the toughest gatekeepers, in any industry: moms! To stay focused on their plan and unwavering with their daily schedule, Marine recruiters regularly tap into one of their fourteen leadership traits: *enthusiasm*. It is half of the battle but can easily be drained when selling.

The right environment is critical for rejuvenating team members and delivering results. While they may put in up to sixteen hours per day, recruiters rely on this essential trait. Not just so they can sell, but so they can maintain the highest energy levels while delivering the results expected of them. Even through fatigue, stress, and frustration, they remain upbeat.

How do they do it? In the heart of every Marine, there beats a connection to their culture, the environment in which they operate. So important to their success, in both recruiting and combat, the Marines gave their culture a name: *Esprit de Corps*. French for the Spirit of the Corps, it unifies their people, no matter what circumstances they face.

Does your sales culture have a name? Does your environment provide you and your team with the internal fortitude to stay on course, the enthusiasm needed to accomplish your sales goals? Culture has been vitally important to humans for thousands of years, and a quick search on Google proves it. There are 794,000,000 results for *culture*.

Unique cultures exist around the world and they have been a powerful tool for human identity, behaviors, and survival since the dawn of mankind. Every sales organization has its own unique sales culture - the environment in which selling occurs (or doesn't). It is also a powerful tool for sales identity, behaviors, and survival. If you search Google, specifically for *sales culture*, there are more than 18,000,000 results.

That's a lot to sift through. So, let's break it down in its most simple terms. Your *sales culture* is the environment in which your people perform. By taking a closer look at the definition of *culture*, we will successfully create the environment necessary for high levels of sales combustion and enthusiasm.

cul•ture
noun

- The set of shared attitudes, values, goals.
- The integrated pattern of human knowledge, belief, and behavior.
- The set of values associated with a particular field.
- The characteristic features of everyday existence shared by people.

In my book, *The LEADERSHIP Connection*, I dedicate Chapter 2 strictly to culture. Titled, *Developing a Unifying Culture*, each page details how leaders can create and maintain an environment that will unite their teams. With the same focus, sales leaders will ignite their sales engines.

THE LEADER'S ROLE

Sales leaders can drive great sales results or drive away great salespeople. Leaders who maintain an environment of high-energy and transformational results are able to retain talented sales professionals and accomplish their goals. Those who ignore the importance of their environments, will often experience unforeseen engine troubles.

Most sales leaders agree that culture impacts performance, but struggle to measure it, impeding their ability to improve it. It is easier to measure tangible sales performance, such as revenue, calls, and appointments. But culture is much different. As an intangible, it can be challenging to assess the strength of your sales environment through simple metrics.

Sales Spark:
All of the greatest sales strategies will not save a weak sales culture.

There are dozens of ways to classify your sales environment: inside sales and outside sales, competitive and cooperative. There are creative, collaborative, profit-driven, and people centric cultures. At the media company, we were a solution-based culture, with a combination of outside and inside sales activities. People were at the core of our business, but we also ensured a healthy bottom line.

Like most sales teams, you probably have a combination of multiple culture-types, which can add to the complexity of assessing your environment and making the necessary improvements. I have found that every culture, regardless of its classification, can be "felt" easier than assessed.

ASSESSING CULTURE

Most sales people are not great at hiding their feelings, especially in the office, so the signs about their environments are all over if you are looking for them. Stepping into any sales department, I can feel the culture that the team operates in and I quickly gauge everything, from their skills and enthusiasm to their anxieties and frustrations. Every sales environment falls into two distinct categories, which I describe with variations of "Ego."

2 Types of Sales Cultures:

- ME-GO - the individual is the priority
- WE-GO - the team is the priority

The ME-GO Sales Environment serves as a more self-centered style, where the individual salesperson is concerned solely or mainly with their own personal results. But spin the "M" in ME-GO 180 degrees and we have the complete opposite. The WE-GO Sales Environment is an altruistic and unselfish style. Below are the signs for both types of sales cultures:

ME-GO Sales Culture:	**WE-GO Sales Culture:**
• *Negative Attitudes*	• *Positive Attitudes*
• *Departmental Walls*	• *Departmental Synergy*
• *Individualism*	• *Teamwork*
• *Consistent Mistakes*	• *Consistent Excellence*
• *High Turnover*	• *High Retention*
• *Internal Rivalries*	• *Internal Collaboration*
• *Low Enthusiasm*	• *High Enthusiasm*

While sales results occur in both environments, the WE-GO culture yields greater, consistent long-term results. Which one do you currently have? Which one do you need to grow your results?

The Sales WE-GO Assessment provides a deeper look into our sales engine. These five categories allow us to gauge the strength of our environment and make the enhancements required to foster a culture of growth, opportunity, and success. Score each part on a scale of 1-10, 10 being best.

Attitudes: Does your sales team bring their A-game, every day?

Synergy: Do all company departments work together for the greater purpose of your organization?

Teamwork: Does your sales team work together as a cohesive unit?

Excellence: Are your products and services being delivered correct and on time, every time?

Retention: Are you keeping your best team members/top producers?

Sales WE-GO Assessment:

What are You Growing?		Rank (1-10)
A	Attitudes	_____
S	Synergy	_____
T	Teamwork	_____
E	Excellence	_____
R	Retention	_____

A.S.T.E.R.

An *aster* is a type of robust flowering plant, that can grow in hazardous environments.

What is growing in your sales environment?

With a possible score of 50, where did your rank your sales environment? Most sales teams fall between 25-30 when they first assess their environments. Allow your sales team to take the assessment to find out how they feel about the culture they operate in. Imagine the possibilities if you could raise each category by one point. Imagine your results.

As the vice president of the media company, I did not take our sales environment lightly. When I started to put together our sales structure, I would have ranked us at 23 out of 50. We had a lot of room for growth and if we were serious about doubling sales, we needed our environment to score higher before we could expect our sales results to grow.

DYNAMIC SALES ENVIRONMENT

We could not afford to have a culture built on egos, so enhancing our sales environment became a top priority for me. As I like to say, "Ego, must go!" And it did. In its place were two primary components that were essential for our culture. To experience consistent sales combustion our environment needed to achieve two outcomes consistently.

2 Outcomes of Sales Culture:

- Powerful Energy
- Predictable Results

When a sales environment fails to deliver these two aspects, it is like driving your sales vehicle up a steep, slippery slope. You feel like you are waging an uphill battle and your sales engine may be at risk of overheating.

Powerful Energy: Energy is the fuel that drives teams to greatness. Sales professionals perform better when they operate in a positive and exciting environment. The collective passion of an enthusiastic sales team will create a new level of energy and your team will feed off of it.

Most sales leaders attempt to create high energy, but the key is to make it sustainable, not sporadic. Contests, incentives, and team building activities are all great for creating high energy. But one factor is essential.

Predictable Results: This is where the rubber meets the road. Are you able to deliver the results promised to the buyer? In most organizations, it is a hit or a miss, with an accepted level of failure that occurs too often in their environments. As I state in *The LEADERSHIP Connection*, "Your culture is exactly at the level of your tolerance for poor performance."

Does the current level of tolerance for mistakes prohibit your team from achieving dynamic sales combustion? If the answer is "Yes," you must enhance your sales environment. When you think about mistakes, put them in the perspective of air traffic control. How many mistakes are tolerated? How many planes were we allowed to crash each day?

The answer is always zero and their environments support that critical objective. Does yours? Without predictable results, culture holds little meaning. We cannot afford to tolerate mistakes because they significantly drain the energy from our sales teams. We all want to deliver results, but we need them to be predictable.

Sales Spark:
In sales, we provide our clients with excuses or results, not both.

THE CAKE

A sales leader's speeches alone, no matter how motivating and inspiring, will not create a high-performance environment for long. It's all lip-service if we fail to deliver results. You may have the most amazing products, spectacular services, and the strongest client relationships. But none of that matters if you cannot keep your promise and deliver the "cake."

Why do politicians rank at the lowest levels of trust? They regularly fail to deliver on their campaign promises. Voters pay attention. So do buyers! Most sales people promise their clients "the world," but struggle to always deliver. A sales environment must allow us to keep our promises.

"Cake" is the criteria that is universal among our buyers. It is what they expect, every time. What is the "cake" for the Marine Corps? Their promise is to, "Make Marines, win our nation's battles, and develop quality citizens." They do not take their promise lightly and their environment supports it at every level. What promises do you make to your clients?

Sales people do not like breaking promises to their clients and if they feel that they cannot deliver predictable results, they may start holding back. This realization became crystal clear to me as we began to focus on our sales environment at the media company. Even the slightest glitch, on a single frame of video, would result in a complete rejection of an order.

In broadcast media, you cannot afford mistakes. But we had them. Because 15% of our orders had errors, I knew it was holding our sales team back. They did not want to be left with egg on their faces if a promise was broken to a client, and I did not blame them. It was a priority to identify our "cake," so we could predictably deliver it.

Sales Spark:
Salespeople sell to the exact level of their perceptions about the capabilities of their support team.

So, I drove our sales vehicle right into the storm and put together a Think Tank session with our key leaders. This collaborative gathering had one purpose: to identify our "cake." What common denominators did every single one of our clients share? We put everything on the table. If something helped us to land a client or keep a client, it was written down.

Our list quickly grew, but the majority of these factors ended up being "icing" on the cake. Sure, they were sweet and tasty, but they were not required by every client. Below is a list of our icing, the elements that improved our sales results, but were not needed in each selling scenario.

The ICING on the CAKE:

- *Special Pricing/Terms*
- *Volume Discounts*
- *Gifts*
- *Lunches/Dinners*
- *Great Customer Service*
- *An Account Executive*
- *Free Vaulting*
- *Free Delivery*

Cookies were also part of our icing. Yes, cookies! We had an Otis Spunkmeyer oven and we baked batches of hot fresh cookies daily. As odd as it may sound, some clients did not want cookies, so this went on the icing list, too. So, what was left? After removing all of the icing from the table, just two things remained - the ingredients for our cake!

The CAKE:

- *Complete Every Order Correctly*   • *Deliver it On Time.*

Every single client wanted the same two things: complete their orders correctly and deliver them on time. If we were correct and late, we failed. If we were on time and incorrect, we failed. Our success would be based on the promise to deliver the cake: correct and on time - every time. Our sales environment was enhanced to support these two factors, with high energy and predictability. Everything else was *icing on the cake.*

Sales Spark:
Never cover up a deficiency in your cake, with extra icing.
Design an environment that produces a better cake.

At Think GREAT our cake is to engage teams and empower leaders.

YOU REAP WHAT YOU SOW

Are you harvesting a bountiful sales yield or are you stuck in the weeds of excuses? Nearly every sales leader believes that their sales teams are capable of producing more. And nearly every sales professional admits to having more potential. The possibilities seem limitless, but your environment needs to support your desired results. You reap what you sow.

Galatians 6:7 states that, "whatsoever a man soweth, that shall he also reap." In other words, what you do will come back to you. At the media company, what I did was focus on our sales environment. What came back to me? The sales combustion that led to more than 300% growth, the elimination of nearly every mistake, and the personal and professional development of our entire team. We delivered for our clients. A bountiful harvest came back, and it will for you, too.

What if your sales environment produced the following?

- Remove all excuses from your sales team
- Have every company leader work together to support sales goals
- Break down the walls between departments
- Eliminate the "Us vs. Them" mindset
- Unify each department and form one cohesive team
- Exceed all sales goals
- Create powerful energy
- Deliver predictable results

Is your current sales environment fostering this level of performance? How would it feel to accomplish one or two of these? What would your results be like if you achieved them all? It feels GREAT! A culture that grows this type of teamwork is within your grasp. But you need to form the team.

SALES SUPPORT TEAM

Sales professionals are the anglers, fishing for the new clients and new opportunities that sustain each business. But every time they step away from the end of the dock, they minimize their true potential. Most sales professionals, to their detriment, attempt to accomplish everything on their own. The go-it-alone approach is not only ineffective, but it often causes more damage than value.

If we expect our sales teams to exceed possibilities, we must position them for success. Our sales support team needs to be in position to handle the entire catch, process them efficiently, and deliver them predictably. In most sales organizations, there is ambiguity and hesitation in the transitioning of the fish (new clients and new orders) to the dock.

Anytime sales professionals stop casting their lines, the momentum of the entire sales operation is in jeopardy. They can easily spend too much time processing an order, doing data entry, setting up a new account, or gathering additional information for an order. I know what you may be thinking, "This is part of my commitment to my client." Or, "This is how I show them I care." Or, "I just wanted to make sure it was done right."

Having a sales support team on the dock is critical to your growth. It keeps sales professionals working "On" their sales goals, while the support team takes the work "In." Your environment needs to keep anglers fishing!

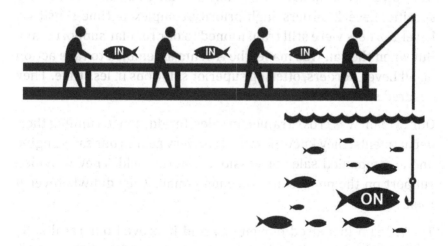

The transition from sales professional to the sales support team is critical. In most sales environments, it is different for each sales person. The strongest sales environments remove excuses and obstacles, eliminating the perceptions that the angler is also a dock worker. Any time anglers stop casting their lines, the fish may soon go to your competitor's dock.

In addition, a significant amount of errors stem from sales people, who notoriously lack the proper information required for success. Our dock identified both the transition point and the criteria (data required), for successful teamwork and transitions. Having a support team also communicates a commitment to the client. Our sales people were part of a team.

THE A-TEAM

As our volume grew and the complexities of our orders increased, we made one significant enhancement to our environment. We created a specialized sales support team, comprised of a diverse team of subject matter experts. We rallied our best leaders, each highly proficient in our systems and services, and we gave them a name - The A-Team.

Our sales professionals were able to call them into action for specific "Level 2" orders: high-priority, complex, or time-sensitive. Level 1 orders were still transitioned to our regular support team. But when the call was made, the A-Team assembled to take action on all Level 2 orders, offering superior solutions in less time. They ensured success.

Our A-Team was cross-trained in sales. In addition to running their departments, they knew how to turn every gear in our sales engine and accompanied sales professionals in the field. They provided support on the phones and through e-mail. They did whatever it took.

The A-Team increased our energy and improved our results. So critical to our success, we had a poster made up of the A-Team, with each of their pictures on it, just like the TV show ads. They even had their own page in our sales manual to describe what they brought to the table (page 193).

The A-Team

ELITE SALES SUPPORT TEAM

They love it when a plan comes together!

Members of The A-Team may be called upon to ensure that all Level 2 orders are completed correctly and delivered on time!

The A-Team is a small team of leaders who have proven the ability to simultaneously accomplish 2 major things:

1. Flawlessly perform their job descriptions

2. Provide unparalleled sales support

We have established dedicated Team Members to handle the coordination and orchestration of Level 2 orders. Just as you must master the System to ensure that your orders are successful, A-Team members must master the Sales Manual to ensure that their sales support is successful.

A-TEAM SALES SUPPORT

Job Specifications	- Media Director
Team Member Involvement	- VP of Operations
Deck Status/Deck Rental	- Operations Director
Labeling Requirements	- Labeling Supervisor

Members of the A-Team will be involved in Think Tank meetings as necessary to coordinate all Level 2 orders. Your communication will be crucial to the success of each Level 2 order. A-Team Members can assist you in strengthening your relationships with your clients. Utilize the A-Team to develop media solutions as you complete and implement bids and proposals to your clients. All great things are accomplished as a team!

PIT-STOP INSPECTION

Sales professionals who operate in a lackluster culture may generate some sales, but not nearly as much as sales professionals who perform with dynamic sales combustion. Every sales person has a great amount of untapped potential and a high-performance sales engine will help to unleash it. But your engine will require regular intervals for fine-tuning.

The pit stops of an automobile race have become one of the most crucial strategies of the race. After all, a car traveling at 200 miles per hour will travel approximately 300 feet per second. So, during a ten-second pit stop, your competition has the ability to gain nearly one-half mile over your "parked" car. The Pit Crew closely examines each racecar before they blast back onto the track.

It is essential that your Sales Pit Crew checks the status of your sales engine every 90 days to ensure that its performance is up to speed. In sales, a Pit-Stop Inspection is a critical strategy that allows us to adjust and upgrade our engines. It provides us time to regroup and refocus our teams.

This is a perfect opportunity to review your plan with the leaders supporting it and assess the strengths and weaknesses of your sales professionals. A Pit-Stop Inspection is essential to prepare everyone for the next 90 days by making any necessary tweaks, so you can accomplish the goals in your next 90-Day Race.

The Pit-Stop Inspection is best used with your sales team, sales support team, and your A-Team. Their collective thoughts and insights will allow your sales engine to perform at the highest levels and will guarantee that your sales vehicle is constantly moving (or flying) in the right direction.

Sales Spark:
Slow down to speed up!

PIT-STOP INSPECTION

Gauge the status of your sales engine after each 90 days. Did you accomplish your three sales goals? Below that, rank the performance and results of your team, using a scale of 1-5, 5 being best. Lastly, write down the performance issues your sales engine encountered, and the adjustments required to fine-tune it for your next 90 days.

Goal #1 Accomplished	☐ Yes ☐ No
Goal #2 Accomplished	☐ Yes ☐ No
Goal #3 Accomplished	☐ Yes ☐ No
Sales Team Performance	1 2 3 4 5
Sales Support Performance	1 2 3 4 5
Powerful Energy	1 2 3 4 5
Predictable Results	1 2 3 4 5

Engine Performance Issues Encountered:

_____

_____

_____

Adjustments Required for Optimal Performance:

_____

_____

_____

TRANSFORMATIONAL GROWTH

The secret of sales success is not a secret. It has been idle, resting under the hood of your sales vehicle the entire time. Creating and enhancing your sales engine is an exciting time. Not only will it drive superior sales results, it will encourage your entire team to raise the bar on their personal performance and pursue new goals.

Dynamic Sales Combustion will produce transformational sales results. You are going to achieve higher energy levels in your sales team and your clients will experience predictable results. Your engine will become a tool for explosive growth, but it functions best when the proper elements are present. Below is the formula for the explosive fuel required for combustion. Make sure you and your team are well-stocked.

Positive Perceptions

+

Laser-Focused Actions

+

Intense Accountability

=

Transformational Sales Results

When you have it, GREAT things happen. Now, imagine the empowering sales meetings that will take place as the fuel flows and your team pushes the limits of your sales vehicle. All you need is a combustible agenda. Every morning, our sales team gathered with the A-Team and our sales meetings did more than merely exchange numbers.

We did not show up to "check the box off" that we conducted a meeting. Our sales meetings served a far greater purpose. They were not only for our sales team, they were for our support team. Our sales meetings were an integral part of our sales environment but lasted only thirty minutes.

They became the breeding ground of growth, success, and teamwork. Our meetings were never just meetings. They followed a simple but effective agenda that unleashed high levels of enthusiasm to start each day.

The Sales COMBUSTION Meeting:

- Personal Vision Statements
- Success Stories
- Goal Status
- Projections & Support
- Training & Development

Each powerhouse meeting started with our sales team and A-Team members, reading their Personal Vision Statements. It was inspirational to hear and understand the greater purpose of our team members. To increase our energy and belief levels, we then shared the successes we experienced and how to duplicate them. This was a confirmation that our sales system was working and encouraged everyone to stay at the end of the dock.

Next up, was a brief status update about our goals. Because our sales engines were firing at such high levels, we were typically ahead of schedule with our goals. If we were behind, we were able to identify the issues and adjust accordingly to get each goal back on track.

We dedicated most of the meeting time to announcing our projections. We discussed the upcoming orders, projects, and new accounts that required strategizing. The A-Team was particularly attentive during this part of the meeting and ready to jump into action, especially as Level 2's were brought up.

But my favorite part of each Sales Combustion Meeting was the training and development section. This is where we "shared the podium." Each day, a different team member prepared and conducted the training on sales skills or product knowledge. They also shared their insights on leadership development and how we could each improve as leaders.

Perhaps the most successful strategy was to include the A-Team in each sales meeting. It transformed our meetings, causing each sales professional to strive for higher levels of performance. With the other leaders in attendance, and taking notes on how to support each sales person, none of them wanted to be left putting up "0's."

Being involved in each meeting was also hugely beneficial for the members of the A-Team. They developed a better understanding of their colleagues in the sales department. They forged deeper friendships, built camaraderie, and supported the company Flight Plan. They were all-in!

THINK GREAT AND IGNITE

Was it exciting to see so much sales combustion? Absolutely, but the highlight of the entire experience was not just creating a revolutionary new sales system. It was not the increased revenue and income. It was watching the team develop. We may have started as a group of media geeks, but we transformed into a dynamic team of 3-Dimensional Sales Leaders.

I never thought I would be in sales, but now I can never imagine myself not in this field. When we do more than just sell, we have the opportunity to impact lives. As you reach that level of sales combustion, something truly dynamic happens. An incredible transformation occurs in your people. I watched it transpire right before my eyes at the media company and I see it in the sales people I coach.

Sales Spark:
When your sales engine achieves combustion, you will move more than your sales vehicle. You will move people!

With the success of each 90-Day Race, our team grew, personally and professionally. Each team member developed and grew in three key areas. I call this transformation the P3 Phenomenon.

The P3 Phenomenon
Passionate • Prepared • Professional

How would you feel if your sales team exuded more passion? What if they were not just ready for success, but prepared to achieve it? What if they increased their professionalism and represented your organization at the highest possible levels? *Dynamic Sales Combustion* provides much more than a better sales system. It allows you to develop the people around you in ways you never imagined.

This journey is about dedicating yourself to continuous self-improvement. It is about making progress, not perfection. Stay focused on consistent learning and development and you will drive your sales performance and results to new and exciting destinations. Like any new action you take, you will experience three phases of growth.

The 3 Phases of Every New Action:

1. Awkward

2. Mechanical

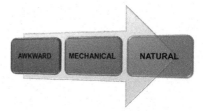

3. Natural

Your sales vehicle is now ready for a dynamic driver. It's time to buckle up, turn the key, and ignite your sales engine. Step on the gas, leave your competition in the dust, and drive your results across the finish line. The checkered flags are waving, and the winner's circle awaits!

It is time for *Dynamic Sales Combustion*!

Acknowledgments

My Deepest Gratitude

This book would never have ignited without the support of the following people. I am eternally grateful for the impact you have made in my business - in my life.

Gina, you were there when I started in sales and you have helped make this journey, and this book, possible. It is exciting to be on this ride with you.

To Erika, you are more than my Executive Assistant, you are the best daughter I could ever ask for. You always have my back and I am so grateful for you.

To Sandy Crosby, you have dynamically "shared" Think GREAT with so many people and have always done it with the highest levels of belief and passion. You have helped so many people to Think GREAT. You are an integral part of this team and our future.

To Saphire Gilpin, you are such a GREAT team member. Your unwavering support, dedication and commitment to our team and our clients is unparalleled. You are an integral part of this team and our future.

To Derek Wetmore, words cannot express my gratitude for your expertise and professional advice. Your enthusiasm for working on this book inspired me and helped to make it greater.

To my clients, thank you for your unwavering trust in me and the concepts in this book. Together, we have been on an incredible journey of sales combustion. You have opened your doors and welcomed me into your businesses as an extension of your team and for that, I am beyond appreciative.

ABOUT THE AUTHOR

ERIK THERWANGER

Erik Therwanger began his unique career by serving in the U.S. Marine Corps as an air traffic controller. Leadership, honor, and integrity did not end after his four-year tour of duty; they became the foundation of his life, both personally and professionally.

After receiving the news that his wife had been diagnosed with cancer, Erik left his job in the entertainment industry, became her caregiver and started his new career in sales.

With no formal training, he began selling financial services. Relying on the strategies and techniques he learned as a Marine, he quickly became a top producer, recruiter, and trainer.

Erik returned to the entertainment industry and became the vice president of a media company in Santa Monica, CA. By building leaders, designing their strategic plan, and creating a dynamic sales system, he helped to raise annual sales by over 300%.

Erik's passion for helping others led to the creation of Think GREAT®. He successfully blends his leadership skills, his unparalleled ability to inspire and develop teams, and his wide array of strategic planning and sales experience, to provide practical solutions for individuals and organizations.

The Three Pillars of Business GREATNESS™ brings together the concepts from *The LEADERSHIP Connection, ELEVATE,* and *Dynamic Sales Combustion to* provide business leaders, and their teams, with a shared language of *leading, planning,* and *selling.*

Sharing his personal story and elite strategies, Erik's keynote speeches inspires audiences to strive for new levels of greatness. His interactive and powerful workshops highlight his step–by–step process for increasing results.

Erik delivers a compelling message that leaves a lasting impact in organizations, creating the necessary momentum to develop strong leaders, build visionary teams, and elevate sales results.

As the author of the Think GREAT® Collection, Erik has combined his challenging life experiences with his goal–setting techniques, to provide proven strategies to enhance the lives of others.

As a trainer and speaker for the spouses of armed services personnel, Erik is deeply aware of their challenges and sacrifices. To help support their education goals, Erik founded the *Think GREAT Foundation,* which is dedicated to awarding scholarships to the MilSpouse community. For more information, please visit:

www.ThinkGreatFoundation.org

www.ThinkGreat90.com

Please visit our website for more GREAT tools:
- Erik Therwanger's Keynote Speeches
- Workshops and Seminars
- Online Training Tools and Videos
- Register for the FREE Great Thought of the Week

More life-changing books in

- The LEADERSHIP Connection
- ELEVATE
- The GOAL Formula
- The SCALE Factor
- GSP: Goal Planning Strategy
- The Seeds of Success for LEADING
- The Seeds of Success for PLANNING
- The Seeds of Success for SELLING

Printed in the United States
By Bookmasters